OUTDOOR SCIENCE SCIENCE LAB *for* *kids*

OUTDOOR SCIENCE LAB *for kids*

52 FAMILY-FRIENDLY EXPERIMENTS
FOR THE YARD, GARDEN,
PLAYGROUND,
AND PARK

QUARRY

Brimming with creative inspiration, how-to projects, and useful information to enrich your everyday life, Quarto Knows is a favorite destination for those pursuing their interests and passions. Visit our site and dig deeper with our books into your area of interest: Quarto Creates, Quarto Cooks, Quarto Homes, Quarto Lives, Quarto Drives, Quarto Explores, Quarto Gifts, or Quarto Kids.

© 2016 Quarto Publishing Group USA Inc.
Text © 2016 Liz Lee Heinecke
Photography © 2016 Quarto Publishing Group USA Inc.

First published in 2016 by Quarry Books,
an imprint of The Quarto Group,
100 Cummings Center, Suite 265-D,
Beverly, MA 01915, USA.
T (978) 282-9590 F (978) 283-2742
www.QuartoKnows.com

Quarry Books titles are also available at discount for retail, wholesale, promotional, and bulk purchase. For details, contact the Special Sales Manager by email at specialsales@quarto.com or by mail at The Quarto Group, Attn: Special Sales Manager, 401 Second Avenue North, Suite 310, Minneapolis, MN 55401 USA.

10 9

ISBN: 978-1-63159-115-0

Digital edition published in 2016
eISBN: 978-1-63159-183-9

Library of Congress Cataloging-in-Publication Data
Names: Heinecke, Liz Lee, author.
Title: Outdoor science lab for kids : 52 family-friendly experiments for the
   yard, garden, playground, and park / Liz Lee Heinecke.
Description: Beverly, Massachusetts : Quarry Books, an imprint of Quarto
   Publishing Group USA Inc., 2016. | "2016 | Audience: Ages 7+. | Audience:
   Grades 4 to 6.
Identifiers: LCCN 2016003845 (print) | LCCN 2016004751 (ebook) | ISBN
   9781631591150 (flexibound) | ISBN 9781631591839 ()
Subjects: LCSH: Science--Experiments--Juvenile literature. | Science--Study
   and teaching (Elementary)--Activity programs. | Science projects--Juvenile
   literature.
Classification: LCC GE115 .H45 2016 (print) | LCC GE115 (ebook) | DDC
   507.8--dc23
LC record available at http://lccn.loc.gov/2016003845

Design, Cover Design, Page Layout: Leigh Ring //www.ringartdesign.com
Photography: Amber Procaccini Photography // www.aprocacciniphoto.com

Printed in China

CONTENTS

INTRODUCTION

THE GREAT OUTDOORS IS NATURE'S OWN SCIENCE LAB, TEEMING WITH POSSIBILITY. When we turn off the screens and head out the screen door, we're immersed in an environment that encourages exploration. Whether it's sunny or snowing, there's always something new to discover.

Writing this book was an adventure that stretched from the last snow of spring to the colorful foliage of early fall. The kids and I spent hot summer afternoons hiking through shady woods. Cornstarch frescos adorned our sidewalks. We used a funnel and garden hose taped to a ladder to turn an empty air mattress into a waterbed. Curious neighbors stopped by to see what we were up to, and one foggy night I dragged the entire family on a moonlit nature hike.

As we experimented our way through the fifty-two labs, projects too messy for the kitchen proved perfect for the driveway, and picnic tables served as lab benches for mixing up lip balm and super spheres. My kids and their friends had a blast blowing huge bubbles and made foaming slime in the backyard. Finding a water bear in tree moss proved to be a challenge, but once we got the hang of it, we were able to observe several of the amazing creatures wiggling under our microscope's lense.

Some of the experiments, such as making an aluminum foil boat for kiddie pools, were perfect for the younger set, while my middle schoolers gravitated toward the more involved experiments. Collecting earthworms was a huge hit, and we were all astonished by the tricks you can do with supercooled water. As we explored, we discovered that a magnifying glass and science notebook enhance any outdoor experience.

Spending time outside had fitness benefits as well—it's hard to sit still when you're searching, collecting, and experimenting. Even our eye muscles got a workout every time we looked into the distance. Peering at moss through a magnifying glass and wading barefoot into a lake gave us a new perspective and reconnected us to the natural world.

Some days it took a fair bit of prodding to get my kids outside, but it was well worth the effort. Nothing compares to exploring our amazing planet with the smell of the seasons and the wind in your hair. Whether you have all day to explore a nature center, or an hour to spend at the playground, or just want to hang out in the driveway, the labs in this book will help you kick off some outdoor science fun of your own.

ABOUT THE LABS

This book will introduce you to fifty-two fun science projects you can do outside. A few have steps that are better suited for a table, such as peering at pond water creatures through a microscope, but they're all meant to be tackled outdoors.

Because several labs involve ecosystems and their inhabitants, you'll have to pay attention to the ebb and flow of seasons to find the best projects for any given day. While many of the experiments are best suited to warmer months, there are some you can do in the snow and several you can bring inside on a cold or rainy day.

Each experiment includes an easy-to-understand explanation of the science behind the project to introduce you to the vocabulary and ideas you're exploring. The labs are set up to make science exploration as simple as following a recipe, with sections detailing the following:

• MATERIALS

• SAFETY TIPS & HINTS

• PROTOCOL (INSTRUCTIONS)

• THE SCIENCE BEHIND THE FUN

• CREATIVE ENRICHMENT

The *Materials* section lists all the ingredients you'll need to conduct each experiment. *Safety Tips & Hints* gives you some common-sense guidelines for doing the experiments. Protocol is a scientific word for instructions, and each *Protocol* takes you step-by-step through the basics of the experiment. *The Science Behind the Fun* offers simple scientific explanations for each experiment, while *Creative Enrichment* gives you variations or ideas for taking the project a step or two further, ideally inspiring you to come up with more questions and ideas on your own.

For kids, the process of experimentation is as important as the results, and it's essential to allow them the freedom to dive in. Measuring, scooping, stirring, digging in the dirt, and getting wet are all part of the outdoor science experience. Wading barefoot into a cool stream to collect samples creates a physical connection to the environment, making any aquatic project memorable.

Some equipment that may prove handy for these labs includes a magnifying glass, duct tape, binoculars, a funnel, and a very basic microscope.

My kids and I worked our way through all of these experiments, and most will turn out well if you follow the protocol closely. However, some may involve tweaking, practice, and innovation. Patience also comes in handy when studying the natural world. Mistakes and troubleshooting are far more educational than perfection, and many scientific blunders have led to great discoveries.

Science Journals

Scientists keep notebooks and journals to document and detail studies and experiments. The scientific method involves asking a question, making observations, and performing experiments that address the question. It's fun to make a science journal to track your own adventures in science.

To make a science journal, find a spiral notebook or composition book or staple some blank pieces of paper together and write your name on the cover. Include a field journal section in your notebook for observing animal and arthropod behavior. Use the field journal to record the date, time of day, location, temperature, weather, and soil conditions. The back pages of your science notebook can be used as a nature log to keep track of the plants, animals, and rock formations you spot when you're out experimenting.

To use the scientific method, write down the following information for each experiment you do:

1. When did you start the experiment? Write the date at the top of the page.

2. What do you want to see or learn? Pose a question. For example, "What will happen when I mix baking soda and vinegar together in a bottle?"

3. What do you think will happen? Build a hypothesis. A hypothesis is a tentative explanation for an observation, phenomenon, or scientific problem that can be tested by further investigation. In other words, it's a guess about what might happen based on what you already know.

4. What happened when you did the experiment to test your hypothesis? Record the results you observe, including data such as measurements and temperature, by writing down, drawing, or photographing your results. Tape photos into your journal.

5. Did everything go the way you thought it would? Look at the information you've collected (your data) and draw a conclusion. Were the results in line with what you thought would happen? Did they support your hypothesis?

After you've done the initial experiment, think of other ways to address the question you asked, try some of the enrichment activities, or invent a new experiment based on what you just did. How can what you learned be applied to the world around you? Jot down your thoughts in your science journal.

UNIT 01
CAPTIVATING CREATURES

FROM MICROSCOPIC PLANKTON TO THE GIANT WHALES THAT DEVOUR THEM, THE DIVERSITY OF CREATURES ON EARTH IS ASTONISHING, AND THERE ARE FASCINATING LIVING THINGS EVERYWHERE YOU LOOK.

While some living things are able to simply duplicate their DNA and divide, others have developed more complicated ways to reproduce. Animals that undergo metamorphosis experience dramatic developmental changes, allowing them to transition from one habitat to another. While tadpoles move from water to land, caterpillars transform, unfurl their wings, and take to the air as butterflies.

Tiny tardigrades, nicknamed water bears for their bearlike claws, don't undergo metamorphosis but are extreme survivalists that can dehydrate themselves to withstand extreme heat, cold, radiation, and even outer space.

Every scoopful of sand or muck from a pond or stream is teeming with an enormous variety of life. From ferocious dragonfly larvae to pinching crawfish, you'll be amazed at what's hiding under the pebbles and twigs.

Carefully capturing and observing living things is a great way to glean insight into the fascinating creatures sharing our world. As you do the labs in this unit, keep in mind that every living animal houses an entire microbial community of its own, so it is essential to release each organism where it was captured to avoid spreading disease from one population to another.

LAB 01

MACROINVERTEBRATE MARVELS

MATERIALS

→ Very fine mesh kitchen sieves or mesh screen food cover

→ White bowls or trays

→ Strainer with larger mesh, or piece of screen (optional)

→ Plastic spoons, forceps, or tweezers for picking up invertebrates

→ Bowl or bucket

→ Empty ice cube tray

→ Magnifying glass

→ Identification key

SAFETY TIPS & HINTS

— Never leave small children unattended near water.

— Assist small children in collecting invertebrates.

— Find a shallow spot where it's easy to wade in at the water's edge.

USE KITCHEN STRAINERS TO COLLECT, SORT, AND IDENTIFY FRESHWATER INVERTEBRATES FROM A LAKE, POND, OR STREAM.

Fig. 4: Observe invertebrates with a magnifying glass.

PROTOCOL

STEP 1: Scoop up sand and mud from the water's edge using a kitchen sieve with very fine mesh. (Fig. 1, 2)

STEP 2: If you don't have a second screen or colander, dump your sample into a white bowl or onto a white tray and watch for movement. (Fig. 3)

STEP 3: If you have a screen or strainer with larger holes, prop it up over the white bowl or tray and dump the muck onto the larger mesh. Wait about 10 minutes. Some invertebrates will drop through the screen on their own onto the surface below. Dump the remaining muck into a second white container.

STEP 4: Gently collect invertebrates from your samples using spoons, forceps, tweezers, or your fingers. Place larger invertebrates, such as snails, clams, or crayfish, in a bowl or bucket with some lake, pond, or stream water. Smaller invertebrates may be sorted into ice cube trays.

STEP 5: Observe the invertebrates with a magnifying glass. Record how many legs each has, and where they are located. Draw them in your science notebook. Record how the invertebrates move around and any unusual features. (Fig. 4)

STEP 6: Use a macroinvertebrate identification key, like the one you can download at stroudcenter.org, to attempt to identify some of the creatures you've captured.

STEP 7: Release the invertebrates in the same spot where you captured them.

Fig. 1: Scoop up some muck.

Fig. 2: Scoop up some more muck.

Fig. 3: Dump your sample into a white bowl.

CREATIVE ENRICHMENT

1. Do you live near the ocean? Try doing a macroinvertebrate study in the sand by the surf.

2. Capture macroinvertebrates using a net in a stream or other running water. Do you see the same creatures you find in the mud at the water's edge?

3. Dig up some dirt and sift it through a screen. What soil macroinvertebrates do you find?

THE SCIENCE BEHIND THE FUN

They may not have backbones, but macroinvertebrates can be fierce. Dragonfly larvae, for example, can even take down tadpoles and minnows.

Macroinvertebrates are defined as animals without backbones that can be seen without using a microscope. Clams, snails, worms, and crayfish are included in the category, but the most abundant macroinvertebrates are aquatic insects. These creatures play an essential role in ecosystems, consuming algae and plants before going on to become food for larger carnivores and omnivores in the food chain, such as fish.

Some scientists do regular macroinvertebrate surveys in their research because the diversity and numbers of macroinvertebrates tell us about water quality and the health of an ecosystem.

WATER BEAR HUNT

MATERIALS

→ Lichens and moss, gently scraped from trees

→ Bottled water

→ Petri dish

→ Microscope

SAFETY TIPS & HINTS

— Collect plenty of lichens and moss.

— Young children will need help finding the tardigrades but will love observing them through the microscope.

— Don't get frustrated if you don't find a tardigrade on your first attempt. If you keep looking, you will find one!

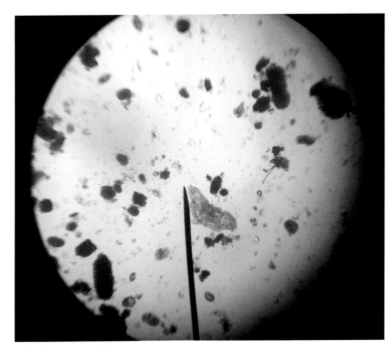

SEARCH FOR TINY TARDIGRADES LURKING IN MOSS AND LICHENS.

Fig. 5: Tardigrades look a bit like caterpillars or strange pigs.

PROTOCOL

STEP 1: Go on a walk and search for moss and lichens on trees. Moss is often green and velvety, while lichens look more like blue-green or blue-gray crinkled crust growing on tree bark. Gently scrape moss and lichens into a container and bring them home. (Fig. 1)

STEP 2: If the moss and lichens are dry, partially cover them with bottled water and let them sit overnight. If they're damp and soft, partially cover them with bottled water and soak them for 5 or 10 minutes. (Fig. 2)

STEP 3: When you're ready to look for tardigrades, gently remove the moss and lichens from the water and shake them over a petri dish, collecting the drops of water in the dish. Squeeze excess water from the moss into the petri dish to form a shallow layer of water. (Fig. 3)

STEP 4: Observe your water sample with a microscope, using the lowest power. It may help to wait a few minutes for everything to settle to the bottom of the petri dish. Look for things that move and are somewhat transparent and pink. (Fig. 4)

Fig. 1: Search for lichens, like the ones in this photograph, and moss growing on tree bark.

Fig. 2: Soak the moss in bottled water.

Fig. 3: Shake and squeeze water from the moss into a petri dish.

Fig. 4: Search for tardigrades using a microscope.

STEP 5: You can distinguish tardigrades from other living organisms by their four pairs of legs. They look a bit like caterpillars or strange pigs. (Fig. 5)

STEP 6: Once you find a tardigrade, center it in the field of vision and increase the magnification for a closer look.

STEP 7: Try to take a picture or video of the tardigrade or draw it in your science journal. See page 141 for a link to a video we made of one of the tardigrades we found.

CREATIVE ENRICHMENT

Collect moss and lichens from the ground and trees. Where do you think you'll find more tardigrades? Test your hypothesis, using your science journal to record your results.

THE SCIENCE BEHIND THE FUN

Tardigrade means "slow walker," but *water bear* is another name for these tiny marvels. Fresh water, salt water, and terrestrial (land-dwelling) versions of these tough creatures are found almost everywhere. Terrestrial tardigrades often live in moss and lichens, which provide a nice, damp environment.

If their habitat gets dry, tardigrades dry out along with it, losing up to 97 percent of their body weight and becoming a dried-out husk, called a *tun*. In this cryptobiotic state, tardigrades can survive almost anything, including extreme heat, cold, chemicals, and even the radiation of deep space. Just add water to rehydrate and reanimate them.

Tardigrades are only half a millimeter long, which is why you need a microscope to get a good look at them. They are different enough from other life forms that they have their own phylum on the tree of life, somewhere between arthropods (such as insects) and nematodes (tiny worms).

LAB 03

TADPOLE TRANSFORMATION

MATERIALS

→ Water containers, such as jars

→ Fish net or bucket for catching tadpoles

→ Larger container to use as habitat

→ Green lettuce boiled for 5 minutes in bottled water and finely chopped (tadpole food)

SAFETY TIPS & HINTS

— Never leave young children unattended near water.

— Never use tap water for your tadpole habitat because chlorine can kill tadpoles.

— Always follow local regulations regarding natural resources and release frogs and toads in exactly the same place you captured the tadpoles to prevent the spread of disease and nonnative species. Never capture tadpoles unless you can return them to the same spot where you caught them!

Fig. 2: Put your tadpoles in chlorine-free water.

WATCH TADPOLES SHAPE-SHIFT INTO FROGS AND TOADS.

PROTOCOL

STEP 1: Check regulations for capturing tadpoles in your area. See whether you can spot some tadpoles in a puddle, fountain, lake, or pond. If local regulations prevent you from catching them, you can keep checking tadpoles to watch them develop in their natural habitat.

STEP 2: If you see tadpoles in the water, collect some of the water in your container. Gently net a few tadpoles and carefully place them in the container. Collect more water and some algae for future use to keep your habitat healthy for the tadpoles. (Fig. 1, 2)

STEP 3: Find a large container with a cover or make a cover from a screen. Make sure there are air holes so the tadpoles can breathe. Create a tadpole habitat using the water and algae you collected, including raised areas like rocks for frogs or toads to hop onto when they're mature. (Fig. 3)

STEP 4: Place the tadpoles in the habitat and observe them every day, adding more water as needed. Make sure some raised, dry areas remain in the habitat.

STEP 5: Every other day or so, feed the tadpoles some tadpole food made from boiled lettuce.

Fig. 1: Gently net a few tadpoles.

Fig. 3: Create a habitat for the tadpoles.

Fig. 4: Return the frogs or toads to the place where you caught the tadpoles.

Fig. 5: Look how much the tadpoles have changed!

STEP 6: Draw your tadpoles every few days in a notebook. Eventually you'll see legs grow and the tails disappear as they move through metamorphosis.

STEP 7: When your tadpoles hop out of the water, return them to the place where you caught them, so they can find food. (Fig. 4, 5)

CREATIVE ENRICHMENT

Keep a metamorphosis journal detailing when the tadpoles are most and least active and how many days it takes for them to form back legs and front legs and to lose their tails. Do they all develop at the same rate?

THE SCIENCE BEHIND THE FUN

It can be advantageous for animals to occupy a different environmental niche than their offspring. While water-dwelling tadpoles are herbivores that eat mostly algae and plants, many frogs and toads hang out on dry land, eating insects and other animals. This means the adults aren't competing for food or space with their kids.

Once they emerge from the egg and begin to eat and grow, tadpoles go through a process called *metamorphosis*, which literally means "changing form." They develop lungs, they grow rear legs and front legs, their tails disappear, and their mouths widen as they mature into frogs and toads.

Frog and toad metamorphosis can take from two months for small toads to two years for larger species, such as bullfrogs, which grow into extremely large tadpoles before going through metamorphosis.

BUTTERFLY GARDEN

MATERIALS

→ Local plants that butterflies are known to lay eggs on, such as milkweed and dill in North America

→ Cup or vase partially filled with water

→ Foil or plastic wrap

→ Large covered container

→ More butterfly-friendly plants or seeds for local plants to put in your garden (optional)

SAFETY TIPS & HINTS

— The best way to pick up a butterfly is by gently pinching its closed wings between your thumb and index finger.

— If you absolutely must move the chrysalis from its perch, firmly wrap and tie a piece of thread around the tiny stem at the top, carefully remove it, and hang it in a safe spot. Be extremely careful not to drop it.

Fig. 6: Plant butterfly-friendly plants in your garden.

OBSERVE THE MIRACULOUS TRANSFORMATION FROM CATERPILLAR TO BUTTERFLY.

PROTOCOL

STEP 1: Research which plants butterflies are known to lay eggs on in your area and look for pictures of butterfly eggs. Search the undersides of leaves for butterfly eggs and caterpillars. Butterfly eggs are very tiny, about the size of a pinhead, and are usually lightly colored. (Fig. 1)

STEP 2: If you find an egg or caterpillar, leave it on the leaf and take the entire stalk of the plant home. Collect more stalks and leaves of the same kind to feed your caterpillar. (Fig. 2)

STEP 3: Put the stem of the plant in a cup or vase containing some water, with foil or plastic wrapped tightly around the bottom of the plant and vase so the caterpillar won't fall in and drown. Place the plant in a larger container with a cover, such as a piece of screen.

STEP 4: Watch the egg hatch and the caterpillar grow. Replace the plant if it dies or all the leaves are eaten. (Fig. 3)

STEP 5: Check the caterpillar every day until it hangs upside down and turns into a chrysalis. As long as you give it fresh leaves, it will get all the water and nutrients it needs from the plant. (Fig. 4)

STEP 6: When the butterfly emerges, leave it alone for at least one day. It has to hang upside down to pump fluid into its new wings. (Fig. 5)

Fig. 1: Search for eggs and caterpillars.

Fig. 2: If you find an egg or caterpillar, take the entire plant stalk home and put it in water.

Fig. 3: Watch the caterpillar grow.

Fig. 4: The caterpillar will turn into a chrysalis.

STEP 7: Release the butterfly.

STEP 8: Plant butterfly-friendly flora in your yard to find more caterpillars next year. You may even help a species survive by providing a place for them to lay their eggs. (Fig. 6)

Fig. 5: Let the newly emerged butterfly hang upside down.

CREATIVE ENRICHMENT

Keep a journal of your caterpillar's growth and development. Measure it every day and record how long it takes to emerge from the chrysalis.

THE SCIENCE BEHIND THE FUN

In the wild, only about 5 percent of monarch butterflies make it from egg to winged wonder; but when you bring them inside, there's a better chance they'll survive to adulthood.

Caterpillars grow at an astonishing rate. Imagine going from the size of an eight-pound (3.6 kg) baby to the size of a cement truck in two weeks, eating only plants, and you'll get the picture. It's even more amazing to watch them transform from fat, wriggling caterpillars to lantern-like chrysalis to majestic, delicate butterflies as they undergo metamorphosis.

Butterflies lay many eggs. Female monarchs, for example, lay about four hundred eggs each on milkweed plants. They're particular about where they set their offspring down, however, and each egg is laid on a different plant or at least a different leaf. This shows you why it's so important for butterflies to have plenty of plants to lay their eggs on.

UNIT 02
DRIVEWAY PHYSICS

IT'S FUN TO MAKE THINGS FLY THROUGH THE AIR. Designing and assembling water rockets attached to produce-bag parachutes is a great way to explore aeronautical engineering. Backyards and driveways are perfect venues for testing other simple physics concepts as well, including centripetal forces, the Bernoulli effect, and even optics. And if you want to play with projectiles, you can make a catapult.

Catapults were first invented as tools of war. The earliest catapults, called *ballistas*, were like giant crossbows. Mangonel catapults have long wooden arms with buckets at the end, and the tension is stored in a rope. Trebuchet catapults were designed to inflict maximum damage using a heavy counterbalance to launch projectiles that destroyed castle and city walls. Warriors flung a multitude of deadly objects at and over fortress walls, including stones, flaming chemicals, and burning tar.

This unit shows you how to make a smaller, less destructive version of a mangonel catapult in your own driveway, using a chip-bag clip and some paint sticks, but don't stop there! Can you figure out how to use rubber bands to make a slingshot for firing marshmallows, or engineer a cardboard box aircraft catapult for launching paper airplanes?

PRODUCE-BAG PARACHUTES

MATERIALS

→ Scissors

→ Empty 12 x 12-inch (30.5 x 30.5 cm) produce bag or other lightweight bag

→ Glue dots

→ String, yarn, or embroidery thread

→ Duct tape

→ Empty 34 fluid ounce (1 L) bottle

→ Ball inflation needle

→ Cork that fits snugly in the mouth of the bottle, cut in half widthwise to form two smaller corks

→ Bike pump

→ Water

→ Safety goggles

→ Shoe box or similar container

SAFETY TIPS & HINTS

— Safety goggles should be worn when shooting off water rockets.

— An adult should cut the cork in half and put the inflation needle through it.

DESIGN AND CONSTRUCT PRODUCE-BAG PARACHUTES TO SLOW THE DESCENT OF A WATER ROCKET YOU SHOOT SKY-HIGH USING A BIKE PUMP.

Fig. 4: Shoot your rocket into the air to test the parachute you made.

Fig. 1: Tape the parachute strings to the bottom of the bottle.

Fig. 2: Push a ball inflation needle through a cork and attach it to a bike pump.

Fig. 3: Add water to the rocket.

PROTOCOL

STEP 1: Cut a produce or other lightweight bag into a 12 x 12 inch (30.5 x 30.5 cm) square to use as a parachute.

STEP 2: Cut four pieces of string, yarn, or thread, each about 12 inches (30.5 cm) long. Use glue dots to firmly attach one string to each corner of the parachute.

STEP 3: Use duct tape to firmly attach the parachute strings to the bottom of a plastic bottle. (Fig. 1)

STEP 4: Push the ball inflation needle through the cork and attach the needle to the bike pump. (Fig. 2)

STEP 5: Fill the bottle about a fourth of the way up with water and plug it tightly with the cork attached to the bike pump. (Fig. 3)

STEP 6: Put your safety goggles on and set the plastic bottle rocket in a container, such as a shoe box, so the bottom of the bottle is pointing up and away from you.

STEP 7: Pump air into the rocket with the bike pump until you have lift off. (Fig. 4)

STEP 8: If your experiment didn't work the way you hoped it would, reengineer your parachute and try again!

THE SCIENCE BEHIND THE FUN

As air pressure builds in the bottle, it pushes the cork and water down toward Earth, which sends the rocket in the opposite direction. Gravity pulls the empty bottle back to Earth, but the open parachute attached to it has a large surface area, which increases air resistance and adds a huge amount of drag to the falling rocket, slowing its fall.

The shape of the parachute, the length of the strings, and even the material the parachute is made from all affect how air moves around it and how well it is able to slow the fall of an attached object. Adding holes to the parachute to help control air movement can also affect how well it works.

CREATIVE ENRICHMENT

1. Change the shape and design of your parachute. What happens if you add holes or more strings?

2. Add different amounts of water to your rocket to see how high it will fly.

CRAZY CATAPULT

MATERIALS

→ 3 or more wooden paint stirring sticks

→ Spring clamp, such as a chip-bag clip

→ Wire

→ Duct tape

→ Nails

→ Hammer

→ Sturdy piece of wood or wooden box

→ Paper cup, with the top two-thirds cut off

SAFETY TIPS & HINTS

— Never use your catapult to shoot projectiles at a person.

CONSTRUCT A MINI CATAPULT FROM PAINT STICKS AND SPRING CLAMPS.

Fig. 2: Tape a paper cup to the upper arm of the catapult.

Fig. 1: Nail the two overlapped sticks to a wooden board or box.

Fig. 3: Add an object to the cup and pull the arm back.

Fig. 4: Release the catapult arm.

PROTOCOL

STEP 1: Securely attach one paint stick to each handle of the spring clamp using wire and duct tape. The sticks essentially lengthen the spring clamp, forming a large *V* with the clamp at its point.

STEP 2: Place the third paint stick so that it lies lengthwise along one end of the *V* and nail the overlapped sticks to a wooden board or box, leaving the other end of the *V* sticking up into the air. (Fig. 1)

STEP 3: Tape the paper cup to the top of the stick in the air to make a launcher for the catapult. (Fig. 2)

STEP 4: Place a small item, such as a dry bean or a marshmallow, in your catapult, pull the top stick all the way down, and then release it. (Fig. 3, 4)

STEP 5: Launch several items of different sizes and measure how far they travel. Can you predict where the items will land?

CREATIVE ENRICHMENT

Change the length of the arm of the catapult. Do you think a longer arm or a shorter arm will shoot objects farther?

THE SCIENCE BEHIND THE FUN

Catapults are machines created to fling projectiles and were built as weapons of war in ancient times. The catapult in this lab is a version of a *mangonel* catapult. The upper arm is attached to a spring clamp, which is a pivoting point called a *fulcrum*. Whatever you put in the paper cup is called the *load* and has the potential to become a projectile.

When you pull the upper stick down, your muscles do work to compress the clamp, storing potential energy in the spring. Releasing the stick unleashes that potential energy and it becomes kinetic energy—the energy of motion. The arm and the load move up quickly, but the spring has limited range of motion and the arm stops fast. The laws of physics say that an object in motion wants to remain in motion, and the load continues to move up and out at the angle at which it was released. Eventually, gravity brings the projectile back to Earth. The path it travels is called its *trajectory*.

LAB 07   CARDBOARD-BOX PROJECTOR

MATERIALS

→ Cell phone or electronic tablet

→ Shoe box (for cell phone) or large cardboard box (for tablet)

→ Magnifying lens or magnifying sheet

→ Cutting tool

→ Tape

→ Box or table, to set up projector

→ Flat white surface, for the screen

Fig. 5: Enjoy the show!

ENGINEER A VIDEO PROJECTOR FOR YOUR PHONE OR TABLET USING A BOX AND A MAGNIFYING LENS.

SAFETY TIPS & HINTS

— This project requires some cutting with sharp tools and may be better for older kids.

— A homemade projector will not produce high-definition images because hand-held devices don't emit enough light, but this is a fun way for kids to learn a little science and watch videos.

PROTOCOL

STEP 1: Turn the light setting and volume on your device all the way up.

STEP 2: Set your phone or tablet down against one end of the box, flush with the cardboard, and mark where the top of your device touches the box.

STEP 3: Line up the top of your magnifying lens or sheet with your mark on the box, trace it, and cut a hole slightly smaller than the size of your magnifier. Cut the opening so that when you place your device on the opposite side of the box, the center of your device will line up approximately with the center of your magnifier. You may have to remove the lens from the holder of a magnifying glass to center it. (Fig. 1)

STEP 4: Tape the lens into the hole you cut. If you are using a magnifying sheet, be sure that the grooved side faces in and the smooth side faces out. (Fig. 2, 3)

STEP 5: Lock the portrait orientation on your phone, so the image can't flip, and open a photo to focus on.

STEP 6: Test your projector when it's dark outside or in a dark room. Turn the device upside down, placing it in the box on the side opposite the lens.

STEP 7: Set your projector on a box or table and focus your image on a flat white surface, such as a garage door, paper, or a sheet. You will have to play around with the distance between the projector and the screen, depending on the distance between the device and the lens and the magnification. To make the image larger, move the box away from the screen and move your device forward inside the box to get perfect focus. Remember to keep the device screen at a 90-degree angle with the bottom of the box. (Fig. 4)

STEP 8: When you have the focus set, start your movie, secure the device to the back of the box, close the lid, or cover the box with a towel to block out excess light, and enjoy the show! (Fig. 5)

Fig. 1: Cut an opening for the magnifier.

Fig. 2: This is a page magnifier in a box projector.

Fig. 3: This is a magnifying glass lens in a shoebox projector.

Fig. 4: Adjust the distance and focus your image.

CREATIVE ENRICHMENT

1. Can you design a better projector? How does the size of the box affect the image?

2. What happens to the image if you add a second lens to your projector?

3. Can you make an even bigger, sharper image with a laptop that produces more light?

THE SCIENCE BEHIND THE FUN

When light from your device passes through the lens on your projector, it slows and bends to form an identical upside-down image at a focal point on the other side of the lens. This light-warping property is called *refraction*.

Although light travels in a straight line from its source, it changes speed and bends when it passes through a new medium, such as a lens. The shape and thickness of a lens determines how and where it refocuses the light waves. Lenses are designed to bend light to focus images in a specific way. Eyeglasses, telescopes, and microscopes all use lenses to help us see things better.

It's essential to adjust the distance between the device, the lens, and the projection surface to get the focal point just right. Since the lens flips the image, you have to keep the screen on your phone upside down to see the image right side up on the movie screen. The lenses in our eyes flip images too, but our brains correct for the difference, so we never even notice.

LAB 08

SOCK CENTRIFUGE

MATERIALS

→ Four 3- to 4-ounce (85 to 115 g) gelatin snack cups, preferably 2 different colors (e.g., red and green)

→ 20 marbles

→ Duct tape

→ 2 socks

→ Piece of kitchen twine or heavy string about 4 feet (120 cm) long

→ Mouth and neck of a 2-liter bottle, cut off with scissors, or a short plastic tube with about a 3/4-inch (2 cm) diameter

SAFETY TIPS & HINTS

— Marbles are choking hazards, so young children must be supervised.

— If you don't have twine, put the gelatin cups in a long sock and just swing the sock in circles. This option is better for very young kids.

— Do not eat the gelatin.

EXPERIMENT WITH CENTRIPETAL FORCES BY SWINGING A SOCK.

PROTOCOL

STEP 1: Remove the covers from the gelatin cups.

STEP 2: Choose 2 cups that are the same color and cover them with as many marbles as will fit in a single layer. Don't push the marbles into the gelatin. (Fig. 1)

STEP 3: Flip the two remaining cups of gelatin over on top of the cups covered with marbles so that the openings face each other. Tape the cups together with a thin piece of duct tape around the middle, so you can see the marbles. (Fig. 2)

Fig. 3: Swing the gelatin sock in a circle over your head.

STEP 4: Put the taped gelatin cups into the toes of the socks with the same color gelatin closest to the toe of each sock. Record what color gelatin is closest to the toe.

STEP 5: Put the string through the bottle neck or tube and securely tie one sock to each end of the string.

STEP 6: With one sock resting on the ground, grasp the bottle neck or tube with your right hand and hold the string under the bottle neck or tube tightly with your left hand.

STEP 7: Stand up and swing the bottle neck or tube in circles with your right hand above your head, so the sock above it swings in a circle. Use your left hand to control your centrifuge. The string in your left hand will pull up as you swing harder.

Fig. 1: Cover the gelatin cups with marbles.

Fig. 2: Tape the gelatin containers together.

Fig. 4: If you don't have string, make a centrifuge with a long sock.

Fig. 5: See what happened to the marbles you spun.

STEP 8: Swing the sock harder. Spin it around your head as many times as you can. Take a break if you need to, but try not to bang the gelatin cups against the ground. (Fig. 3, 4)

STEP 9: Remove the gelatin from the socks, and observe the marbles. (Fig. 5)

CREATIVE ENRICHMENT

1. Test what happens if you change the amount of weight in the bottom sock. How much weight do you have to add to swing the upper sock in a circle slowly without holding on with your left hand?

2. Make concentration gradients with colored gelatin and test how different-size marbles move through them using your sock centrifuge. Make sure you have the highest density gelatin on the bottom of the cup.

THE SCIENCE
BEHIND THE FUN

If you swung the sock with enough force, you'll notice that the marbles moved into the gelatin nearest the toe of the sock.

On a sharp curve, tires keep your car on the road using the forces of friction. In this case, a string supplies the force to keep the sock holding the heavy gelatin and marbles moving along a circular path. If it weren't for the string, the whole thing would fly off in a straight line!

Inside the sock, the gelatin supplies the force to keep the marbles moving in a circle. However, the marbles are denser than the gelatin, and if you swing them fast enough, the gelatin can't supply enough force to keep them in place and they slowly drift through it, away from the center.

The faster you spin the sock, the more force it takes to keep it going in a circle. The string you hold in your left hand supplies the force it takes to keep your swinging sock from flying straight out, and you can feel it pull up with more force as you swing the sock faster and in wider circles.

THE BERNOULLI EFFECT

MATERIALS

→ Scissors

→ 3 narrow plastic newspaper bags

→ Glue dots or double-sided tape

SAFETY TIPS & HINTS

— Supervise small children around plastic bags.

INFLATE A NEWSPAPER BAG BALLOON WITH A SINGLE BREATH, AS IF BY MAGIC.

Fig. 4: Hold the bag a few inches (8 to 10 cm) from your lips and inflate it with a thin stream of air.

PROTOCOL

STEP 1: Cut the ends off of two of the newspaper bags. (Fig. 1)

Fig. 1: Cut the ends off of two newspaper bags.

Fig. 2: Glue or tape the ends of the bags together to form a single bag.

Fig. 3: Hold the bag up to your lips and try to blow it up.

STEP 2: Glue or tape the three bags together to form a single long bag with the uncut bag forming a closed end. (Fig. 2)

STEP 3: Put the bag to your lips and see how many breaths it takes to inflate it. (Fig. 3)

STEP 4: Now, with someone holding the opposite end of the bag up off the ground, position the bag a few inches (8 to 10 cm) away from your lips and blow a long, steady stream of air into it. If you do it correctly, the bag should inflate with a single breath. (Fig. 4)

CREATIVE ENRICHMENT

Come up with more experiments to demonstrate Bernoulli's principle.

THE SCIENCE BEHIND THE FUN

If you cut a 2 x 5-inch (5 x 13 cm) piece of thin paper and hold it just under your bottom lip and blow, the entire piece of paper will rise. Daniel Bernoulli was a scientist who studied moving fluids, such as liquids and gases. He developed a principle that states that the pressure in a moving fluid is lower in regions where the fluid is moving faster.

When you blow on the paper, the pressure is lowered in the stream of moving air that you make with your breath above the paper. As a result, the pressure below the paper is higher and pushes the paper up. This is the same principle that explains the lift below the wings of an airplane.

In this experiment, you can inflate a long tube of plastic bags by blowing a small stream of air into a bag open to the outside air. Bernoulli's principle tells us that this is possible because the pressure drops where you blow, and air rushes into the bag to fill the area of low pressure surrounding the stream of air created by your breath.

UNIT 03
INVERTEBRATE INSPECTION

IF YOU GO BY NUMBERS, INVERTEBRATES RULE THE WORLD. These spineless marvels make up well over 90 percent of the animal species that have been identified on Earth and include everything from insects and arachnids to snails, worms, and single-celled creatures called *protozoa*.

Some are so small that you can only view them under a microscope, while others, like giant tube worms living near toxic, deep sea ocean vents, can grow to be over seven feet (2.1 m) long.

There are lots of experiments you can do to learn about your invertebrate neighbors. In addition to identifying them, you can observe their behavior and even bring them to the surface to study more closely. You'll find them fascinating.

In this chapter, you'll learn to make a bug house, sweep for arthropods, fish for planaria, and irritate earthworms.

BUG HOUSE

MATERIALS

→ 10 to 20 sow bugs or pill bugs (see *Protocol* for finding and catching them)

→ Jar or other container for bringing the bugs home

→ Rectangular plastic box and piece of cardboard, or 2 half-gallon (1.9 L) cardboard milk cartons

→ Scissors and/or utility knife

→ Duct tape or masking tape

→ Paper towels or dirt

→ Black or brown construction paper

SAFETY TIPS & HINTS

— Adult supervision is required when using a utility knife to cut holes.

— Do not do this experiment with spiders or other insects that can bite or sting. If you live in an area with poisonous snakes, use caution moving rocks and logs while you look for bugs.

CREATE CONNECTED MICROENVIRONMENTS TO LEARN ABOUT PILL BUGS AND SOW BUGS.

Fig. 5: Observe the bugs' behavior.

PROTOCOL

STEP 1: Collect sow bugs or pill bugs from under rocks and pieces of wood. These bugs are ¼ inch (6 mm) to ½ inch (13 mm) long and have seven pairs of legs and a segmented body, like armor. Pill bugs are also called roly polys and can roll up into tiny balls. (Fig. 1, 2)

STEP 2: Cut a snug-fitting piece of cardboard to divide your plastic container in half. Cut a small opening about 2 inches (5 cm) wide into the middle of the bottom of the cardboard for bugs to move through. Tape the cardboard container into place. (Fig. 3)

For milk cartons, cut the tops off, leaving 4 inches (10 cm) on the bottom. Cut identical holes in the side of each carton about ⅓ inch (1 cm) from the bottom. Tape the cartons together so the holes line up to form a single opening. (Fig. 4)

Fig. 1: Collect sow bugs and pill bugs.

Fig. 2: Look under rocks and pieces of wood.

Fig. 3: Make a bug house from a divided plastic container.

Fig. 4: You can also make a bug house from milk cartons.

STEP 3: Add wet paper towels or dirt to one side of the habitat and dry towels or dirt to the other side so the bugs can crawl back and forth easily between the two sides.

STEP 4: Place an equal number of bugs on each side of the habitat and observe them for an hour or so. Every 15 minutes, record how many bugs are on the moist side and dry side of the environment. (Fig. 5)

STEP 5: Repeat the experiment making one side of the habitat dark by covering it with the construction paper, and leaving the other side open to the light. Add an equal number of bugs to each side and see which habitat they prefer.

STEP 6: Release the bugs back where you collected them.

CREATIVE ENRICHMENT

Try creating other microenvironments for the isopods. See what foods they prefer.

THE SCIENCE
BEHIND THE FUN

Every living thing has a preferred environment. Whether it's an aquatic environment such as a lake, where gills are an asset, or a very cold one, where you need antifreeze proteins in your blood to survive, we all have our own specific niche in Earth's ecosystem.

The word microenvironment refers to a small area with specific conditions, like the conditions under a rock in a pine forest, which would probably be cool and damp, with soil underneath and decaying organic matter all around.

Pill bugs and sow bugs belong to the order Isopoda and are crustaceans, with hard, armorlike exoskeletons, requiring them to have segmented bodies and jointed legs to move. They are the only crustaceans that spend their entire lives on land, but like their lobster and crayfish relatives, they have gills and require moisture to breathe. In this experiment, when you put them in a dry microenvironment next to a damp one, chances are they will move toward the moisture.

SWEEP NET ARTHROPOD INSPECTION

MATERIALS

→ Sweep net or materials to make one: pliers; two wire hangers; scissors; an old, light-colored pillowcase; duct tape; and long wooden broomstick or sturdy yardstick

→ Large white piece of fabric, such as an old sheet

→ Jars

→ Insect identification books (optional)

SAFETY TIPS & HINTS

— Don't pick up insects with your bare hands unless you know they don't bite or sting.

— Ticks love tall grass. If there are ticks in your area, take precautions and do a tick check after your insect hunt.

COLLECT AND IDENTIFY AMAZING ARTHROPODS USING A NET YOU CAN MAKE YOURSELF.

Fig. 3: Sweep the grass and plants to catch invertebrates.

PROTOCOL

STEP 1: If you don't have a sweep net, make one by using pliers to straighten two wire hangers and twist them together. Form them into a loop, leaving about 3 inches (7.5 cm) straight on either end. Cut about one third off of the open end of a pillowcase and pull the mouth of the pillowcase over the wire loop, leaving the 3-inch (7.5 cm) extension bare. Tape it securely around the perimeter. To complete the net, tape the straight part of the hangers onto the end of a broomstick or yardstick. (Fig. 1)

STEP 2: Find an area with long grass and plants, such as a meadow or field. Sweep with your net the same way you'd sweep a floor, but flip the open side of the net back and forth to capture insects in the grass. (Fig. 2, 3)

STEP 3: Close your net by flipping the bottom over the top and carry it over to your fabric.

Fig. 1: Make a sweep net from wire hangers and a pillowcase.

Fig. 2: Get ready to sweep.

Fig. 4: Observe your catch more closely in jars.

Fig. 5: Try to identify what you caught in your sweep net.

STEP 4: Carefully release the creatures you've collected onto the fabric to inspect them. If you want a closer look, use a leaf or stick to pick up an insect and put it inside a jar with a loose lid. (Fig. 4)

STEP 5: Count how many legs and body segments they have and look for antennae, wings, and unique color. Record your observations in a notebook.

STEP 6: If you want, you can use insect identification books or other means to identify what you've found. (Fig. 5)

STEP 7: Keep a journal of the insects and arachnids you capture, the time of day, and where you found them.

CREATIVE ENRICHMENT

1. Sweep sections of the same area at different times of day (dawn, noon, dusk, and night) to see how the population changes.

2. Compare what you find in different habitats, for instance, prairie versus marsh.

THE SCIENCE BEHIND THE FUN

Arthropods are amazing animals with skeletons outside their body, called *exoskeletons*, segmented bodies, and jointed legs.

When you sweep, chances are you'll find lots of insects, which are arthropods with six legs. They often have wings, and their life cycle goes from egg to larva to adult. Some insects, such as butterflies, also go through a pupal stage, in which their bodies are significantly transformed. The antennae on their heads are sensory organs.

Insects with similar features are classified into groups such as bees, butterflies, dragonflies, grasshoppers, and beetles.

You may also find some arachnids, with eight jointed legs and exoskeletons. Spiders, ticks, and scorpions all lay claim to this frightening, fascinating class of creatures. Their bodies have only two segments, and they do not have antennae or wings. The pair of legs closest to the head assists them in feeding and self-defense.

FISHING FOR FLATWORMS

MATERIALS

→ Knife that can cut meat

→ Raw meat such as steak or liver

→ String or fishing line with (optional) fish hook

→ Metal sinker or rock

→ Collection container such as a jar

→ Magnifying glass

→ Microscope with a petri dish or slides (optional)

SAFETY TIPS & HINTS

— Never leave young children unattended near water.

— Always wash your hands after handling raw meat.

— If you don't have any luck catching flatworms, look for them on the bottom of large, flat rocks sitting in clear, still water. Use a paintbrush to sweep them into your collection container.

CATCH AND OBSERVE FASCINATING, FREE-LIVING PLANARIA.

Fig. 4: Observe the planaria you catch.

PROTOCOL

STEP 1: Search for a spot, such as a pond, lake, or small stream, to catch flatworms called *planaria*. They prefer shade and still, clean water, often hiding out near docks, lily pads, large, flat stones, and debris. Flatworms are more active at night.

STEP 2: Cut meat into coin-size pieces and tie it to long pieces of string or use it to bait a fishing hook. Add a sinker near the meat or tie a rock on to the string. (Fig. 1)

Fig. 1: Put meat on a string with a weight.

STEP 3: Drop your bait into the water and wait 5 or 10 minutes. Set out more bait in different spots and at different depths while you wait.

STEP 4: Fill a collection container with water from the fishing area.

STEP 5: When it's time, pull the flatworm bait up slowly and lower it into the water in your container. (Fig. 2)

STEP 6: Use a magnifying glass to look for flatworms on the meat. They have a soft, unsegmented, flat body and an arrow-shaped head. If you don't find any flatworms, lower the bait into the water and leave it for 3 to 4 hours before checking again. (Fig. 3)

STEP 7: Observe the planaria you catch with your magnifying glass and under a microscope, if you have one. Draw a planarium in your science notebook and record the behavior you observe. (Fig. 4)

Fig. 2: Pull the bait from the water and put it in a jar.

Fig. 3: Use a magnifying glass to look for flatworms.

CREATIVE ENRICHMENT

1. Study how planaria respond to light.

2. Try to keep your planaria alive by feeding them fish food and changing the water on occasion. They prefer cool temperatures, and chlorine will kill them, so use bottled water.

THE SCIENCE BEHIND THE FUN

Planaria are free-living flatworms with the uncanny ability to regenerate. In fact, if you cut one in half, the head section will grow a new tail, the tail section will grow a new head, and you'll have two planaria swimming around. You can cut them up in any direction and they will form an entirely new body, with everything in the right place.

Flatworms have very basic nervous systems, and most of their sensory organs are located near their heads. When you look at a planarium under magnification, you'll notice that it has prominent eyespots. These aren't true eyes but contain cells called *photoreceptors* to help them sense light.

Lacking a body cavity to hold internal organs, a planarium must eat through an opening on its underside called a *pharynx* and use specialized cells called *flame cells* to remove waste. Planaria are scavengers that feed on decaying organisms and small invertebrates, which explains why you can fish for them using meat as bait.

LAB 13 EARTHWORM ERUPTION

MATERIALS

→ ⅓ cup (48 g) ground mustard

→ 1 gallon (about 4 L) water

→ Empty milk jug, bucket, or other large container

→ String, sticks, or stakes

→ Container for earthworms

SAFETY TIPS & HINTS

— Don't splash the mustard water in your eyes. It will sting!

— We've had the best luck catching lots of worms in grassy yards.

USE GROUND MUSTARD SEED DISSOLVED IN WATER TO MAKE EARTHWORMS WRIGGLE TO THE SURFACE WHERE YOU CAN CATCH THEM.

Fig. 4: Observe the earthworms.

PROTOCOL

STEP 1: Add the ground mustard to the water in the jug, bucket, or large container and stir until dissolved. (Fig. 1)

STEP 2: Measure out a 1-square-foot (30.5 x 30.5 cm) sample plot with string and sticks or stakes.

STEP 3: Pour about half of the water-mustard mixture over the dirt in your grid. (Fig. 2)

Fig. 1: Stir ground mustard into water.

Fig. 2: Pour the water-mustard mix over the ground.

Fig. 3: Catch worms!

STEP 4: Wait for the worms to come up. When they've emerged completely, grab them and put them in a container. (Fig. 3)

STEP 5: When worms stop emerging, add the rest of the mustard mixture to the plot and wait for a second batch of worms to appear from deeper in the soil.

STEP 6: Observe your earthworms. (Fig. 4)

CREATIVE ENRICHMENT

1. Measure out plots in different environments to see how many worms you catch.

2. Identify the worms you find and send them, or report your findings, to a citizen science project (see *Resources*, page 141).

THE SCIENCE BEHIND THE FUN

Long ago, glaciers killed all of the earthworms native to North America above the glacial boundary. As a result, almost all of the earthworms found in the northern United States today are a nonnative species, *Lumbricus terrestris*, brought over from Europe centuries ago in soil used as ship ballast and along with plants. Although they have a reputation for aerating gardens, they can be harmful to woodlands, where they disrupt the duff layer of decomposing material on the forest floor, making it difficult for young plants to take root and grow.

Recently, a new species of worms has come into the mix in North America. Asian earthworms of the genus *Amynthas* are also called jumping worms. They reproduce quickly, and several can live together in one place, causing extensive damage to forests.

To help stop the spread of invasive earthworms, never discard unused fishing worms in forests, compost, or even water. Throw them away in the garbage.

UNIT 04
PICNIC TABLE CHEMISTRY

WE TEND TO IMAGINE CHEMISTRY AS AN INDOOR ENDEAVOR, BUT YOU CAN CREATE CHEMICAL REACTIONS ANYWHERE. Tote kitchen chemicals outside to experiment without worrying about the mess. Set up a stand where neighborhood kids can blow giant bubbles, play with magic orbs, and shop for homemade lip balm while they sip lemonade. You'll have the most popular front lawn on the block.

It's simple to turn a picnic table into a lab bench where you can try oil spherification. After that, mix up some cosmetics chemistry with coconut oil, beeswax, and flavored drink mix to create lip balm. Blowing giant bubbles isn't just fun; it teaches you about surface tension. And if you like mixing baking soda and vinegar together, you'll love making foaming slime.

There's even something for artists in this unit, which teaches you to make simple frescoes using cornstarch, water, and food coloring. True fresco paintings are applied to a damp layer of lime, sand, and clay and can last thousands of years as the result of a chemical reaction, but you can rinse cornstarch frescoes away with a garden hose.

FOAMING SLIME

MATERIALS

→ Unopened 8-ounce (235 ml) plastic water bottle

→ Sheet of paper to make a funnel

→ Detergent containing sodium tetraborate (e.g., Borax)

→ Baking soda

→ Paper cups

→ Glue

→ Vinegar

→ Food coloring

→ Marker

SAFETY TIPS & HINTS

— Supervise young children so they don't put detergent in their mouths.

— Label bottles containing detergent.

COMBINE TWO CLASSIC EXPERIMENTS TO MAKE COLORFUL, BUBBLY SLIME OOZE FROM A BOTTLE.

Fig. 3: Watch the foaming slime emerge.

PROTOCOL

STEP 1: Remove the label from a water bottle, take the lid off, and pour out about 2 ounces (60 ml) of water.

Fig. 1: Add the detergent and baking soda to the water.

Fig. 2: Pour the glue-vinegar solution into the detergent–baking soda solution.

STEP 2: Using a paper funnel, add 1 teaspoon (5 ml) detergent and 5 teaspoons (23 g) baking soda to the water in the bottle. Put the lid back on the bottle and shake well. Label the bottle "detergent-baking soda." (Fig. 1)

STEP 3: In a paper cup or small pouring container, mix together 2 tablespoons (30 ml) vinegar, 2 generous tablespoons (30 ml) glue, and a few drops of food coloring. Mix well with a stick or spoon. If you're using a paper cup, pinch one side to create a pouring spout.

STEP 4: Shake the bottle of detergent-baking soda solution and set it on a tray or plate. Remove the lid from the bottle.

STEP 5: Immediately pour all the glue-vinegar solution into the water bottle very quickly. (Fig. 2)

STEP 6: Watch the chemical reaction create foaming slime. When your bottle has stopped "erupting" foamy slime, squeeze it out of the bottle. (Fig. 3, 4)

Fig. 4: Squeeze the foam out of the bottle.

CREATIVE ENRICHMENT

1. Add more or less water to your glue solution to see what happens.

2. Try adding different amounts of baking soda and vinegar to the reaction.

THE SCIENCE BEHIND THE FUN

Polymers are long chains of molecules, like beads on a necklace. In fact, polymer means "many parts." Glue contains a chemical called *polyvinyl acetate*, a polymer that is runny when you mix it with water or vinegar. However, if you add sodium tetraborate, which is called a *cross-linker,* to glue, all of the glue molecules stick (or link) together in a big glob.

Mixing together baking soda (sodium bicarbonate) and vinegar (acetic acid) creates a chemical reaction that produces carbon dioxide gas.

When you pour glue-vinegar solution into baking soda–detergent solution, the chemical reaction between baking soda and vinegar forms carbon dioxide gas bubbles as glue molecules link together, trapping gas bubbles inside gluey polymer slime. The slime pushes its way out of the bottle as pressure builds inside.

GIANT BUBBLES

MATERIALS

→ About 54 inches (137 cm) of cotton kitchen twine

→ 2 sticks 1 to 3 feet (30.5 to 91.5 cm) long

→ Metal washers

→ 6 cups (1.4 L) distilled or purified water

→ ½ cup (64 g) cornstarch

→ 1 tablespoon (14 g) baking powder

→ 1 tablespoon (20 g) glycerin (Corn syrup may be substituted for glycerine.)

→ ½ cup (120 ml) blue dish detergent (Dawn and Joy in the U.S. work well; try Fairy, Dreft, or Yes in Europe.)

→ Tray

SAFETY TIPS & HINTS

— Use the recommended detergents for the best results.

— This experiment works best on humid days when it's not too windy.

CONCOCT A SURFACE TENSION-BUSTING, EVAPORATION-SLOWING SOAP SOLUTION TO CREATE GIANT BUBBLES.

PROTOCOL

STEP 1: Tie one end of the cotton string to the end of one stick. Put a washer on the string and tie the string to the end of the other stick so the washer is hanging in-between, on around 36 inches (91 cm) of string. Tie the remaining 18 inches (46 cm) of string to the end of the first stick, forming a string triangle. (Fig. 1)

STEP 2: Mix the water and cornstarch. Add the remaining ingredients and mix well without whipping up tiny bubbles. (Fig. 2) (Optional Step: Let the solution sit for one hour; stir gently before using.)

STEP 3: With the two sticks parallel and the washer hanging down in between, completely immerse the string on your bubble wand in the bubble mixture. (Fig. 3)

STEP 4: Carefully pull the string up out of the bubble mixture and pull the sticks apart slowly so that you form a string triangle with a thin layer of bubble mixture in the middle.

STEP 5: Step backwards or blow bubbles with your breath. You can "close" the bubbles by moving the sticks together to close the gap between strings. (Fig. 4)

Fig. 1: Make a bubble wand with sticks, string, and a washer.

Fig. 2: Mix up your bubble solution.

Fig. 3: Dip the bubble wand string into the bubble mixture.

Fig. 4: Make some giant bubbles!

CREATIVE ENRICHMENT

1. What other substances can you add to your bubble solution to prevent evaporation?

2. Make another wand with a longer or shorter string. How does it affect your bubbles?

3. Try different recipes to see if you can improve the bubbles. Do other dish soaps work as well?

4. Can you make scented bubbles, with vanilla or peppermint oil, or will it interfere with your soap layers?

5. Can you figure out how to blow a bubble inside another bubble?

6. Try blowing bubbles in the winter. Do they last longer? Do they sink or rise better than they do on a hot day? Why?

THE SCIENCE
BEHIND THE FUN

Water molecules like to stick together, and scientists call this attractive, elastic tendency *surface tension*. Surfactants like detergent molecules have a hydrophobic (water-hating) end and a hydrophilic (water-loving) end. This makes them very good at reducing the surface tension of water.

When you add dish detergent to water, the lower surface tension allows you to blow a bubble by creating a thin film of water molecules sandwiched between two layers of soap molecules, all surrounding a large pocket of air.

Bubbles strive to be round. The air pressure in a closed bubble is slightly higher than the air pressure outside of it and the forces of surface tension rearrange their molecular structure to have the least amount of surface area possible. Of all three dimensional shapes, a sphere has the lowest surface area. Other forces, like a breeze, can affect the shape of bubbles as well.

The thickness of the water/soap molecule is always changing slightly as the water layer evaporates and light waves hit the soap layers from many angles, causing them to bounce around and interfere with each other, giving the bubble a multitude of colors. Solutions like glycerine and corn syrup slow water layer evaporation, allowing bubbles to stick around longer.

DRIVEWAY FRESCOES

MATERIALS

→ 16 ounces (454 g) cornstarch

→ Scant 1 ½ cups (355 ml) water for painted fresco or 1 ½ cups (355 ml) red cabbage juice (see Note) for an acid-base fresco

→ Tray or pie tin (optional)

→ Baking soda and vinegar for acid-base fresco

→ Food coloring for painted fresco

→ Toothpicks or small paintbrushes

→ Cups

→ Plate

Note: To make red cabbage juice, chop up ½ of a head of red cabbage, cover with water, and boil for 5 minutes. Strain out the cabbage.

SAFETY TIPS & HINTS

— Chopping and boiling red cabbage should be done with adult supervision.

— Food coloring may leave marks on concrete.

CHANNEL YOUR INNER MICHELANGELO BY CREATING A MASTERPIECE ON CORNSTARCH AND WATER.

Fig. 4: Paint your fresco with food coloring.

PROTOCOL

STEP 1: Mix together the cornstarch and either water or red cabbage juice. You can use your hands. The resulting mixture, which will look like glue, is fun to play with. (Fig. 1, 2)

STEP 2: Pour some cornstarch mixture onto a clean, flat spot on a driveway or sidewalk. You can also pour it into a tray or pie tin.

STEP 3: When the mixture has flattened out, let it sit for 5 or 10 minutes before you begin painting on it.

STEP 4: To decorate an acid-base fresco made with red cabbage juice, put vinegar in one cup and a few tablespoons (40 to 55 g) baking soda mixed with ¼ cup (60 ml) water in a second cup. Use toothpicks or paintbrushes to make designs on the cornstarch with the baking soda solution and vinegar. For a painted fresco, put food coloring on a plate and use toothpicks or paintbrushes to paint designs with it on your fresco. (Fig. 3, 4)

Fig. 1: Mix cornstarch and water.

Fig. 2: The mixture looks like glue and is fun to play with.

STEP 5: Let your frescoes dry. What happens as they sit?

STEP 6: Wash your frescoes off the sidewalk using water from a hose.

CREATIVE ENRICHMENT

1. What other household acids and bases could you use to paint on an acid-base fresco?

2. What happens if you let your fresco material (cornstarch mix) dry before you paint on it?

Fig. 3: Paint a cabbage juice fresco with vinegar and baking soda.

THE SCIENCE BEHIND THE FUN

In this experiment, you play with the technique of painting on a wet, plasterlike surface made from a non-Newtonian liquid of cornstarch and water. The substance is called non-Newtonian because it doesn't behave the way we expect a liquid to and acts more like a solid if you stir it around or try to move it quickly.

When you use food coloring to paint, as in an actual fresco, the water-based pigments (color molecules) are absorbed into the cornstarch mixture, but they don't travel far since the cornstarch mixture is so thick.

If you try the acid-base painting, you'll see that vinegar, an acid, makes pink lines, and baking soda solution, a base, makes blue or green lines. The pigment molecule from the red cabbage juice is an acid-base indicator that changes shape depending on pH, absorbing light differently and changing color.

LEMONADE STAND LIP BALM

MATERIALS

→ Microwaveable bowl

→ Coconut oil

→ Beeswax beads or grated beeswax

→ Colorful liquid drink mix drops or water-flavoring drops

→ Small containers with lids to hold lip balm, such as empty contact lens cases

→ Toothpicks or craft sticks for stirring

SAFETY TIPS & HINTS

— Heating and pouring steps must be done by an adult or with adult supervision to avoid burns.

— The beeswax–coconut oil solution can be reheated if it starts to harden before you're ready to pour it into smaller containers.

USE YOUR SIDEWALK AS A CHEMISTRY LAB TO MIX UP SOME LIP MOISTURIZER.

Fig. 4: Make lip balm for your friends.

PROTOCOL

STEP 1: In a microwaveable bowl, mix together 2 parts coconut oil to 1 part wax beads (e.g., 8 tablespoons [112 g] coconut oil, 4 tablespoons [55 g] wax beads).

STEP 2: Microwave the mixture at 30-second intervals, stirring in between, until the wax is completely melted and the solution is clear. (Fig. 1)

STEP 3: Cool the solution very briefly. If it gets cloudy or turns white, you'll need to reheat it.

STEP 4: While the solution cools, add a drop or two of flavoring mix to the lip balm containers.

Fig. 1: Melt the coconut oil and beeswax.

Fig. 2: Mix liquid drink flavoring into the lip balm.

STEP 5: Carefully pour some hot coconut oil–beeswax mixture into one of the lip balm containers and stir with a toothpick. To mix the color in, continue stirring as the lip balm cools into a smooth paste. Repeat until you've filled all of your containers. (Fig. 2)

STEP 6: When the lip balm has cooled completely, smooth it off using a craft stick or the back of a metal spoon warmed in hot water and dried off.

STEP 7: Try the lip balm out. Keep it, give it to your friends, or peddle it at a lemonade stand! (Fig. 3, 4)

Fig. 3: Display lip balm alongside lemonade at your summer stand.

CREATIVE ENRICHMENT

Make up your own lip balm recipe. Research the safety of all extra ingredients and label your lip balm if it contains allergens.

THE SCIENCE BEHIND THE FUN

Scientists at cosmetic companies work hard to synthesize smooth, moisturizing lip balms and cosmetics that look good but aren't bad for your skin. It's tricky to get the combinations just right, and they have to keep a number of other factors in mind, including cost and shelf life.

Coconut oil is actually a mixture of fats and oils that is somewhat solid at room temperature but melts easily when it gets warm. In this lip balm concoction, it serves as a moisturizer called an *emollient*, which acts as a barrier to hold the natural moisture in your lips.

Beeswax melts at high temperatures but solidifies at room temperature, thickening the lip balm. Since oil and water don't mix together easily, and your colorful flavor drops are mostly water, you have to keep stirring them into the cooling wax and oil mixture to form a suspension of tiny globs, called an *emulsion*. Once the lip balm has cooled, the wax helps hold the entire solution together so that the oil doesn't separate out.

SUPER SPHERES

MATERIALS

→ 2 cups (475 ml) vegetable oil in a tall container, such as a jar or glass

→ 1 cup (235 ml) water

→ Five ¼-ounce (7 g) packets unflavored gelatin or 3 tablespoons (24 g) agar powder

→ Saucepan or microwaveable bowl

→ Food coloring

→ Squeeze bottles or empty squeezable glue containers

SAFETY TIPS & HINTS

— Adult supervision is required for microwaving and pouring hot liquids.

— The spheres may be a choking hazard.

— If you're doing this experiment with several kids, it's better to have two or more chilled containers of oil, so you can switch jars if the oil starts to warm up.

MAKE COLORFUL, GELATINOUS ORBS THAT SHRINK WHEN YOU DRY THEM OUT.

Fig. 5: Dry some super spheres on a plate.

PROTOCOL

STEP 1: Chill the vegetable oil on ice or in the freezer until very cold but not frozen. (Fig. 1)

STEP 2: Heat the water in a microwaveable bowl or in a saucepan on a stovetop. Whisk in the unflavored gelatin or agar powder. Continue to microwave or boil on the stovetop as needed, stirring until the powder is completely dissolved. (Fig. 2)

STEP 3: Add a few drops of food coloring to each of your squeezable containers.

STEP 4: Cool the hot gelatin or agar mixture briefly. When cooler but not solid, add some melted gelatin or agar to each of the squeeze bottles. Swirl to incorporate the food coloring.

STEP 5: Remove the cold oil from the freezer or ice.

STEP 6: Slowly squeeze the gelatin or agar solution into the cold oil, a few drops at a time so it forms into marble-size orbs and sinks. Allow them to cool for 30 seconds or so and retrieve with a slotted spoon or strainer after you've made about ten orbs. (Fig. 3)

Fig. 1: Chill the vegetable oil on ice.

Fig. 2: Add the gelatin or agar to the water.

Fig. 3: Drop the gelatin or agar solution into cold oil.

Fig. 4: Make more orbs.

STEP 7: Rinse the orbs with water and repeat, rechilling the oil as needed until you have as many orbs as you want. (Fig. 4)

STEP 8: Dry some of the super spheres by setting them on a plate overnight to watch them shrink. Rehydrate them with water to see what happens. They can be kept in a plastic bag in the refrigerator. (Fig. 5)

THE SCIENCE BEHIND THE FUN

Some chefs use a technique called *oil spherification* to make tiny edible morsels using everything from balsamic vinegar to fruit juice, mixed with gelatin and agar. They call it *molecular gastronomy*, and it takes advantage of the fact that water and oil don't mix. Gelatin and agar are colloids that solidify as they cool, and the water-based droplets falling through chilled oil form perfect spheres due to surface tension.

CREATIVE ENRICHMENT

1. Make floating spheres by making the orb mixture with 1 cup (235 ml) white vinegar and 3 tablespoons (24 g) agar powder. Add the orbs to water containing a few teaspoons (14 to 18 g) of baking soda.

2. Make color-changing spheres by dissolving 3 tablespoons (24 g) agar powder in 1 cup (235 ml) red cabbage juice (made by boiling red cabbage in water). Drop the orbs into vinegar (an acid) or into water containing baking soda (a base).

UNIT 05
BOUNTIFUL BOTANY

MOSSES ARE FASCINATING ANCIENT PLANTS THAT RELY ON SUPPORTIVE NEIGHBORS. Lacking tissue and structures to carry water, they can't grow very tall and so they lean on each other in large groups to form velvety carpets. There is safety in numbers, and life in a mossy mat helps them survive direct exposure to harsh conditions. Moss is one of the few plants that can grow in extremely cold places like Antarctica because it requires little light and can enter a dormant state when things get tough. Scientists have even discovered moss growing under glaciers.

Although they depend on regular exposure to water from rain, fog, and dew for moisture, nutrients, and even part of their reproductive cycle, mosses are able to get around well enough. They find new ground by producing spores that blow in the wind, allowing new mosses to spring up far from the parent clumps.

More complex plants are fun to experiment with too. Besides playing with moss, this chapter is full of ideas to help you explore how plants grow, bloom, find light, and make oxygen.

LAB 19

FLOWERBOX PHOTOTROPISM

MATERIALS

→ Beans, peas, or sunflower seeds

→ Small cups

→ 2 shoe boxes

→ Spare cardboard

→ Scissors or box cutter

→ Duct tape

→ Dirt or potting soil

WATCH PLANTS SEEK THE LIGHT IN THIS A-MAZE-ING EXPERIMENT.

Fig. 4: Check to see how your plants are growing.

SAFETY TIPS & HINTS

— Small children will need assistance cutting the box.

— Beans, peas, and seeds present a choking hazard for young children.

PROTOCOL

STEP 1: Plant 1 or 2 beans, peas, or sunflower seeds in 2 or 3 small cups of dirt. Water them so the soil is damp and let them grow for a few days until you have small sprouts. Water your sprouts again before putting them in the phototropism boxes. (Fig. 1, 2)

STEP 2: Label your first shoe box A, turn it on its side like a diorama, and cut a small hole into one corner of the side that's now facing up.

STEP 3: Label the second shoe box B and set it on one of its short ends, so that it's standing tall. Cut a small hole in a corner of the short end that's facing up.

STEP 4: Cut a piece of cardboard shorter than the width of box B. Duct tape the cardboard into box B on the same side as the hole you cut, about 7 inches (18 cm) from the bottom of the shoe box. It should be positioned so that if you place a plant directly under the hole, the light will be blocked by the cardboard, with enough space next to the cardboard for the plant to grow through. (Fig. 3)

STEP 5: Add one of your cups of sprouts to shoe box A, taping the cup to the box on the end opposite the light hole. Close the box tightly.

Fig. 1: Put dirt in cups.

Fig. 2: Plant seeds, such as beans, peas, or sunflower seeds.

Fig. 3: Make a light maze.

STEP 6: Tape the second cup of sprouts into shoe box B, directly under the light-blocking cardboard so that it will be forced to grow through the opening on the opposite side to reach the light. Close the box tightly.

STEP 7: Set your boxes in a sunny place for several days, checking and watering every 2 days or so. (Fig. 4)

THE SCIENCE
BEHIND THE FUN

The word *tropos* comes from the Greek language and indicates turn, reaction, response, or change. Plants must respond to many different stimuli to grow and survive. They work with the force of gravity to grow roots down into the earth, where water is more likely to be found.

It's also essential for most plants to find light, so they can make energy from light and carbon dioxide. *Photo* means light, so scientists use the word phototropism to describe a plant's tendency to turn and grow in the direction of light.

In this experiment, you plant a seed or two in a box with a single light source and a few obstacles in the way of the light. A plant has enough energy stored in the seed from which it emerges to begin to grow, but you will see that as it gets bigger, it grows around the obstacles to reach the light source.

CREATIVE ENRICHMENT

1. What other experiments could you create to study plant tropisms? How could you test whether roots grow down as they sense the force of gravity?

2. Try making more complex mazes to see how far a plant will grow to reach the light. Which plant species work best in light mazes?

MARVELOUS MOSS

MATERIALS

→ Several clumps of moss gently collected from the ground or carefully scraped from trees and rocks (see Note)

→ Magnifying glass

→ 2 or more containers for growing moss

→ Small rocks or pebbles

→ Spray bottle

→ Potting soil

→ Blender, buttermilk, and paintbrushes for moss paint (optional)

SAFETY TIPS & HINTS

— Supervise kids when blending moss paint.

— It can be tricky to get moss paint to thrive. It should be misted frequently and may take more than a month to grow. Be patient.

— Moss paint may grow best on surfaces similar to where you found the moss growing.

CREATE VELVETEEN GARDENS AND LIVING PAINT FROM THIS ANCIENT WONDER OF THE PLANT WORLD.

Fig. 4: Paint the moss slurry onto different surfaces.

PROTOCOL

STEP 1: Collect moss and observe it through a magnifying glass. Record the appearance of each type of moss and note where it was collected. Divide each moss sample into 2 or more clumps. (Fig. 1)

STEP 2: Place different types of moss in a container filled with small rocks. Add water to the container so that it comes up just to the bottom of the moss but doesn't cover it.

STEP 3: Fill a second container with potting soil and duplicate the first container's planting pattern with a second set of moss clumps. Water the soil until damp but not wet. (Fig. 2)

Fig. 1: Inspect moss through a magnifying glass.

Fig. 2: Plant moss on rocks and on dirt.

Fig. 3: Blend moss with buttermilk.

STEP 4: To make moss paint, blend a large clump of moss with ½ cup (120 ml) buttermilk. Paint moss slurry designs onto different surfaces to see where it will grow best. (Fig. 3, 4)

STEP 5: Mist your moss daily and water the moss base of soil or rocks as needed. Mist the moss paint once or twice a day.

STEP 6: Record the health of your moss and which conditions it prefers in your science notebook.

CREATIVE ENRICHMENT

1. Use tree moss to look for tardigrades (see Lab 2).

2. Duplicate this experiment outdoors, using what you learned to create a healthy moss garden.

3. Add water to dry moss, one drop at a time, and observe what happens under a microscope.

THE SCIENCE BEHIND THE FUN

Scientists have identified more than ten thousand species of moss. Classified as bryophytes, different kinds of moss require different conditions to grow. Mosses hate competition, so you tend to find them growing where other organisms don't thrive, such as on rocks, packed soil, or wood. Some mosses love the sun, while others hide in caves. They lack flowers and true roots but have structures called *rhizoids* that anchor them to surfaces.

Moss lack structures for carrying water, so they must absorb water directly from the environment to survive. They are perfectly formed for collecting and absorbing water and grow in large bunches so they can hold water like a sponge.

In this experiment, you'll test different conditions for growing different types of mosses to see what makes them thrive or wilt. Blending moss with a moist, sticky base to make paint is a fun way to establish a new moss garden on a vertical surface.

PETAL BOMB

MATERIALS

→ Fresh flowers

→ Glue, double-sided tape, or glue dots

→ Large sheets of paper, poster board, or foam board

→ Scissors

SAFETY TIPS & HINTS

— Help small hands by pre-positioning glue dots on paper in concentric circles so kids can easily place petals on the adhesive.

— Remind kids to ask permission before raiding gardens.

DISSECT BLOSSOMS TO CREATE AN EXPLODED VIEW OF A FLOWER.

Fig. 5: Compare exploded flowers.

PROTOCOL

STEP 1: Cut some fresh wildflowers, weedy blooms, or garden blossoms. (Fig. 1)

STEP 2: Starting with the sepal, or small green leaves on the outside of a blossom, pull off flower parts, beginning with the outside layer of petals. Affix the outer leaves and petals paper to paper, foam board, or poster board in a large circle. (Fig. 2)

STEP 3: Continue to remove and glue petals and flower parts, from the outside in, to your paper or poster board in concentric circles, moving toward the middle. (Fig. 3)

Fig. 1: Pick a flower.

Fig. 2: Pull the petals off, from the outside in and stick to paper.

Fig. 3: Make concentric circles of petals, moving towards the middle.

Fig. 4: Identify the parts of the flower.

STEP 4: Glue the middle parts of your flower to the middle of your paper. Put the stem wherever you choose.

STEP 5: Identify the different parts of your flower using an online resource. (Fig. 4)

STEP 6: Compare exploded flowers. (Fig. 5)

CREATIVE ENRICHMENT

1. Try to find some flowers with all male parts or all female parts (hint: think squash).

2. Make an exploded view of a small blossom to press and dry between two sheets of wax paper in a book.

3. Get creative and overlay exploded views of more than one flower, lining up similar parts.

THE SCIENCE
BEHIND THE FUN

Every part of a flower plays an important role in creating seeds. While sepals help protect developing buds, brightly colored petals attract pollinators such as insects, birds, and even bats.

Flowers can have male parts, female parts, or both male and female parts. The male parts consist of long, threadlike filaments that hold up pollen-laden anthers. Female flower parts include a sticky stigma atop a tubelike structure called a *style*, which leads down to the flower's ovary.

When pollination occurs, pollen becomes trapped on the stigma and moves down the style to fertilize the ovule, the part of the ovary that eventually becomes a seed.

Many flowers also produce sweet, nutrient-rich nectar to attract pollinators. Plant pollination is extremely important to humans as well. According to the United States Department of Agriculture, of all the crop plants grown around the world, almost 80 percent require pollination by animals such as bees.

AQUATIC OXYGEN

MATERIALS

→ Common, submerged water plants from a pond or lake

→ Container for transporting the plants

→ Large plastic container

→ Water

→ At least 2 small, clear containers, such as glasses or test tubes

SAFETY TIPS & HINTS

— Never leave young children unattended near water.

— Endangered water plants should not be used.

— Water plants should be composted or thrown away following the experiment.

Fig. 4: Watch for oxygen bubbles to form.

OBSERVE WATER PLANTS MAKING OXYGEN UNDERWATER.

PROTOCOL

STEP 1: Collect water plants. (Fig. 1, 2)

STEP 2: Fill a large container with tap water. If possible, let it sit overnight to remove chlorine. Submerge your small, clear containers and turn them on their sides underwater to remove all the air bubbles.

STEP 3: Cut a branch off of your plant, place it underwater in the large container, shake off any air, and put it under one of your small, clear containers with the stem side up, so that the top of your plant is enclosed. Holding the container with the plant in it underwater, turn the entire thing upside down, allowing no air to enter it (see photo). If you're using test tubes, position them in small cups or beakers so they don't tip over. (Fig. 3)

STEP 4: Invert one small clean container but don't add a plant. This is your control. If you have extra plants and small containers, repeat step 3 to add more samples to your experiment.

STEP 5: Place your experiment in bright sunlight or near a strong lamp for several hours and observe it. You may see oxygen bubbles form on the plants and collect in the clear containers as the plants perform photosynthesis. (Fig. 4)

Fig. 1: Collect water plants.

Fig. 2: Put the plants you collected in a container to take home.

Fig. 3: Submerge water plants under small inverted glass containers.

THE SCIENCE BEHIND THE FUN

Plants are food, but they're also our friends. In fact, we couldn't survive without them.

Our green allies are very good at rearranging chemicals. Using the sun's energy, a light-absorbing green pigment called *chlorophyll*, and a process called *photosynthesis*, plants turn water and carbon dioxide into sugar (glucose) and oxygen. This fuel-rich sugar gives them the energy they need to grow and survive.

Thanks to plants and other organisms such as algae that synthesize their own food from inorganic substances like carbon dioxide using light or chemical energy, Earth's atmosphere contains enough oxygen to keep us alive and well.

CREATIVE ENRICHMENT

1. What happens if you duplicate the experiment in a room with no light?

2. Tap water contains some carbon dioxide. How do you think the experiment would work with lake or pond water?

TINY TREES

→ Pinecones and tree seeds

→ Pan or cookie sheet

→ Tweezers

→ Cup or small container with water

→ 2 clear plastic zip-top bags

→ Sand or peat

→ Paper towels

→ Small rocks

→ Potting soil

→ Small pots

→ Plastic bag

SAFETY TIPS & HINTS

— Growing pine trees from seed takes several months, but you can plant maple seeds that fall in spring and they will grow right away. You can also keep them in the fridge, with pine seeds, if you want a winter science project.

— Seeds present a choking hazard for young children.

SPROUT A SAPLING FROM A SEED.

PROTOCOL

STEP 1: Collect closed or partly closed pinecones and tree seeds, such as maple helicopters, from several trees in the fall. (Fig. 1)

STEP 2: Set the pinecones in a pan or on a cookie sheet to dry out for several days until they open and pine seeds fall out. (Fig. 2)

STEP 3: Collect the remaining pine seeds from the cones using tweezers and put them in a container with some water.

STEP 4: Discard the seeds that float because they may not germinate. Remove the seeds that sink from the water and allow them to dry.

STEP 5: Fill a zip-top bag with moist (not wet) sand or peat (or a combination of equal amounts of the two) and mix the pine seeds in. Close the bag most of the way, leaving a small opening for air. Place the bag in the refrigerator for 3 to 6 weeks.

STEP 6: Remove the maple seeds from their helicopter casings, if you are using them, and put them on a damp paper towel inside another zip-top bag. Seal the bag part way and put it in the refrigerator for up to 8 weeks. (Fig. 3)

Fig. 5: When your trees are big enough to survive, plant them outside.

Fig. 1: Collect pinecones.

Fig. 2: Dry the pinecones so that seeds fall out.

Fig. 3: You can refrigerate maple seeds or try to plant them right away.

Fig. 4: Plant tree seeds in potting soil.

THE SCIENCE BEHIND THE FUN

The seeds from most trees won't sprout, or germinate, right away because they are in a dormant state. Dormant means "as if asleep." To wake up seeds, their thick seed coats must be softened or dissolved in a process called *scarification*.

Since many trees start growing in spring, some seeds must be exposed to cold for a time before they begin to grow. You can trick seeds by mimicking winter, using a process that gardeners call *stratification*. This is why you refrigerate the seeds for several weeks before planting them.

CREATIVE ENRICHMENT

1. What other trees can you germinate from seed?

2. Research and test different methods of scarification on tree seeds.

STEP 7: Check your seeds every week or so. If they start to sprout, remove them from the cold and plant them (see step 8).

STEP 8: When your seeds have completed their stay in the cold, put some small rocks and then a mix of peat, sand, and potting soil in pots. Plant your seeds a few inches (7 to 10 cm) below the surface and water them regularly to keep the soil damp. (Fig. 4)

STEP 9: As soon as your seedlings appear tall and strong enough to survive and it's warm enough to dig, move them outside to their new home. (Fig. 5)

UNIT 06
ATMOSPHERIC AND SOLAR SCIENCE

THE NORTHERN LIGHTS ARE THE STUFF OF LEGEND, ONCE IMAGINED TO BE ANCESTRAL SPIRITS, THE GLOW FROM DISTANT CAMPFIRES, OR OMENS OF WAR AND FAMINE.

Thanks to modern science, we now know that the spectacular lights of the Aurora Borealis are the result of clashing particles rather than clashing titans. Energetic particles, known as the solar wind, regularly escape the sun's gravity and race toward Earth, and massive eruptions on the Sun's surface and solar flares occasionally send huge bursts of these particles our way.

Earth is a giant magnet with magnetic poles near the North and South poles. The magnetic field deflects most of the solar wind around the earth, but some of the particles are trapped by the field and spiral down near the magnetic poles. These energetic particles crash into gasses in Earth's atmosphere, causing oxygen and nitrogen molecules to release light. The color of the light display depends on the type of colliding gas and the altitude where the collision occurs. It can be red, blue, or purple, but green is the color most commonly seen.

In this unit, you'll experiment with energy from the Sun and atmospheric gasses. You can't re-create the Northern Lights, but you can make a cloud in a bottle, use the Sun's energy to pop a balloon, and do a card trick with atmospheric pressure.

SOLAR HEAT BEAM

MATERIALS

→ Balloon

→ Marshmallow

→ Magnifying glass

SAFETY TIPS & HINTS

— This will only work on a mostly cloudless, sunny day.

— Adult supervision is recommended.

POP A BALLOON OR BURN A MARSHMALLOW USING THE SUN'S ENERGY.

Fig. 4: See what the Sun's energy does to a marshmallow.

PROTOCOL

STEP 1: Blow up a balloon. (Fig. 1)

STEP 2: Stand with the Sun behind you.

STEP 3: Holding the balloon in one hand, use the magnifying glass to focus the Sun's light onto the balloon. Move the magnifying glass back and forth until the light is focused into the brightest, smallest spot possible.

Fig. 1: Blow up a balloon.

Fig. 2: Focus sunlight on the balloon until it pops.

Fig. 3: Prop up a magnifying glass to focus sunlight on a marshmallow.

STEP 4: Keep the Sun focused on the balloon until it pops. (Fig. 2)

STEP 5: Set a marshmallow on a plate or the driveway and figure out a way to prop up your magnifying glass to keep the Sun's light focused on the marshmallow. We used an upside-down flower box with a drainage hole. (Fig. 3)

STEP 6: Check on the marshmallow every few minutes. When the marshmallow starts to smoke, take away the magnifying glass. (Fig. 4)

CREATIVE ENRICHMENT

1. Try this experiment using a water balloon.

2. Blow up several balloons of different colors to the same size to see whether color affects the length of time it takes it to pop.

3. Measure the focal length of different magnifying glasses (see *The Science Behind the Fun*).

THE SCIENCE BEHIND THE FUN

Did you know that it is possible to start a fire using very clear ice, formed into a large lens? It's all about the shape.

A magnifying glass is a convex lens, which means that either side of it is shaped like the outside of a bowl. The lens bends light coming through one side of the lens so that all the light rays passing through converge on a single point on the other side. The spot where the light rays meet is called the *focal point*.

If you hold your magnifying glass too far away from the balloon, the spot of light will get bigger and less bright. That's because once the light rays pass through the focal point, they start to spread out again.

The Sun's light waves carry a lot of energy, and they can transfer that energy when they interact with matter. When all the light waves traveling through your magnifying glass bombard the same small point, that energy is able to heat up whatever happens to be sitting in front of it, whether it's a balloon or a marshmallow.

The amount of the Sun's heat you can focus on an object has to do with the size and shape of the lens. Do you think a bigger lens will focus more heat than a smaller one can?

SUN PRINTS

MATERIALS

→ Leaves, flowers, and grasses

→ Colorful construction paper

→ Plastic wrap or large acrylic sheet, such as plexiglass

SAFETY TIPS & HINTS

— This experiment works best on a sunny day when the Sun is directly overhead.

MAKE FRAMEWORTHY ART USING THE SUN TO BLEACH DESIGNS ON PAPER.

Fig. 4: You've made sun prints!

PROTOCOL

STEP 1: Collect flowers and leaves with interesting shapes.

STEP 2: Set some colorful construction paper on a sidewalk or other flat spot in the Sun.

STEP 3: Place your flowers and leaves on the paper in any design. (Fig. 1)

STEP 4: Cover the paper and plants with plastic wrap or plexiglass and weigh it down with rocks if it's breezy. (Fig. 2)

STEP 5: After several hours, remove the plastic and plants from your sun prints. (Fig. 3, 4)

Fig. 1: Put flowers and leaves on the construction paper.

Fig. 2: Cover your items with plastic wrap or clear plastic so they don't blow away.

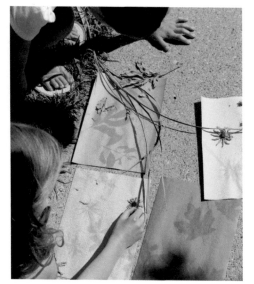

Fig. 3: Remove the plastic and plants to reveal your design.

CREATIVE ENRICHMENT

1. Experiment with different sun exposure times to see how long it takes ultraviolet light to fade the paper.

2. Test whether some colors fade more easily than others.

3. Spray sunscreen on some paper, let the paper dry in the shade, and repeat the experiment to see what happens.

THE SCIENCE BEHIND THE FUN

Earth's own star, the Sun, emits a huge amount of energy, some of which travels to Earth and through the atmosphere as light. This light moves through space as waves, and, like waves on the ocean, light waves can be far apart or close together.

The colors we see around us are the result of visible light waves being absorbed by different objects. Some light waves are too close together to be detected by human eyes. These waves, in the ultraviolet spectrum, have lots of energy and can break down chemical bonds. These chemical changes can permanently change the way objects such as construction paper absorb light, changing their color.

In this experiment, some of the paper is protected from ultraviolet rays because it's hidden under leaves and flowers. When you remove them, you can see that their image remains, while the paper around them has been bleached by sunlight. This illustrates why staying in the shade helps to protect your skin from the sun's ultraviolet rays.

BIKE-PUMP CLOUD

MATERIALS

→ Ball inflation needle

→ Cork that fits the mouth of the bottle, cut in half widthwise

→ Ball pump or bike pump

→ Safety goggles or glasses

→ 2 tablespoons (30 ml) rubbing alcohol (isopropanol) or hard alcohol (ethanol)

→ Clear 2-liter (2 qt) bottle with label removed

SAFETY TIPS & HINTS

— An adult should cut the cork in half and put the inflation needle through it.

— Adult supervision is required for small children. Isopropanol is poisonous if consumed. Avoid inhaling isopropanol fumes from the bottle.

— Safety glasses are required

— Don't overfill the bottle with air. Follow the instructions carefully.

PRESSURIZE A SODA BOTTLE TO CREATE AN INSTANT CLOUD.

Fig. 4: Remove the cork to create a cloud in the bottle.

PROTOCOL

STEP 1: Push the inflation needle through one of the cork halves. It may work best where the corkscrew has gone through.

STEP 2: Attach the needle to the bike pump. (Fig. 1)

STEP 3: Put on your Safety goggles or glasses. Add the alcohol to the bottle and coat the insides of the bottle by rolling it around. (Fig. 2)

STEP 4: Put the cork attached to the pump firmly into the bottle.

Fig. 1: Set up a bike pump with an inflation needle and a cork.

Fig. 2: Coat the inside of a plastic bottle with alcohol.

STEP 5: Feel the sides of the bottle and then begin pumping slowly, with the bottom of the bottle pointed away from you, until the sides of the bottle feel very firm. You will need to hold the cork in the bottle as you pump or have someone else pump while you hold the cork in place. (Fig. 3)

STEP 6: With the bottom of the bottle pointed away from you, remove the cork. You should see a white cloud in the bottle. (Fig. 4)

STEP 7: Return the cork to the bottle and pump until the sides feel firm again. The cloud should disappear.

STEP 8: Remove the cork.

Fig. 3: Pump air into the bottle.

CREATIVE ENRICHMENT

1. Are there other liquids you could use for this experiment?

2. Will plain water work?

THE SCIENCE BEHIND THE FUN

Alcohol evaporates quickly at room temperature, becoming an invisible gas. However, cold alcohol molecules can stick together to form tiny alcohol droplets, creating a fog that you can see.

In this experiment, you increase the pressure in an alcohol-coated bottle by pumping in more air. Some of the alcohol in the bottle has already turned to gas by the time you start pumping. The trapped gas molecules, water molecules, and air molecules in the bottle get pushed very close together as the pressure rises, causing the temperature in the bottle to go up.

When you remove the cork, the pressure drops very rapidly, and the temperature inside the bottle also falls fast. This causes the alcohol molecules and some water molecules to condense into droplets, forming a cloud inside your bottle.

If you put the cork back in and pump air in, the pressure goes back up, the temperature rises, and the molecules become invisible gas again.

FLIPPED WATER GLASS

MATERIALS

→ Glass with a mouth small enough to cover with a playing card

→ Deck of playing cards

→ Water

SAFETY TIPS & HINTS

— The cards may be damaged by water.

— Small children may need assistance with this experiment.

TIRED OF THE SAME OLD CARD TRICKS? ASTONISH YOUR FRIENDS WITH THIS IMPRESSIVE INVERSION EXPERIMENT.

Fig. 4: Atmospheric pressure holds the card on the glass.

PROTOCOL

STEP 1: Add some water to your glass. Make sure the glass is only partially full so that there is still some air on the top. (Fig. 1)

STEP 2: Cover the mouth of the glass completely with a playing card. Don't leave any gaps and keep the card flat. (Fig. 2)

Fig. 1: Pour water into your glass.

Fig. 2: Cover the glass with a playing card.

STEP 3: Put one hand flat over the card, being careful not to bend the card, and quickly invert the glass. It might be easier to use your fingers instead of your palm.

STEP 4: If no water is leaking out, remove your hand from the card. The card should remain on the mouth of the glass, holding the water in. (Fig. 3, 4)

STEP 5: If you have a leak, try again! You may need a new card.

Fig. 3: Flip the glass over and take your hand off of the card.

CREATIVE ENRICHMENT

1. Add more water to the glass. How much water can you add?

2. Put dish soap around the edge of the glass. Do you get the same results?

3. Make pin holes in the card and repeat the experiment. Does the water leak through the holes? Why or why not?

THE SCIENCE
BEHIND THE FUN

We live at the bottom of an ocean of air molecules. Although we don't notice it, these molecules push on our bodies and everything around us with a powerful force called *atmospheric pressure*. This pressure pushes on us from all directions.

When you flip the covered water glass over, water molecules in the glass are pulled down by gravity. However, the force of the water pushing down is lower than the force of atmospheric pressure pushing up on the card, so the water stays in the glass.

Surface tension is at work as well, since water molecules like to stick together, forming an elastic-like skin at their surface. Some water molecules even stick to the card due to another force called *adhesion*, which helps hold the card on the glass.

If your friends ask, just tell them that atmospheric pressure provides enough push to keep the card on the glass and that surface tension and adhesion help stop leaks.

ULTRAVIOLET WAVE DETECTOR

MATERIALS

→ 2 clear glasses, cups, or jars

→ Tonic water

→ Tap water

→ Dark piece of paper or fabric

SAFETY TIPS & HINTS

— This experiment works best in bright sunlight.

USE THE SUN'S ULTRAVIOLET LIGHT TO MAKE TONIC WATER GLOW.

Fig. 4: You may notice that the tonic water glows faintly and has a bluish hue.

PROTOCOL

STEP 1: Fill one cup with tonic water. (Fig. 1)

STEP 2: Fill the second cup with tap water. (Fig. 2)

STEP 3: Set the cups side by side indoors or in a heavily shaded area. Hold the dark paper behind the two cups and compare the color.

STEP 4: Set the two cups side by side in the Sun and hold the dark paper behind them. You may notice that the tonic water glows faintly and has a bluish hue. (Fig. 3, 4)

Fig. 1: Add tonic water to a clear cup.

Fig. 2: Add tap water to a second cup.

Fig. 3: Set the glasses of water in the sunlight.

STEP 5: Now repeat the experiment in a lightly shaded area directly adjacent to a sunny one.

STEP 6: Record your observations in your science notebook.

CREATIVE ENRICHMENT

1. What else can you use to detect ultraviolet light? Try Lab 25, Sun Prints.

THE SCIENCE BEHIND THE FUN

Our eyes can detect visible light waves, but some light waves, such as infrared, are too long for us to see. Other light waves in the ultraviolet spectrum are too short for our eyes to see. The Sun's ultraviolet rays are the same ones that can burn your skin, and although they're invisible, they still carry a lot of energy.

Tonic water contains the chemical quinine, which is also used to treat malaria. Quinine has the ability to absorb the ultraviolet light from the sun and re-emit the energy as visible light. This process is called *fluorescence,* and it's a useful tool in many science labs. Tap water does not contain any special fluorescent molecules, so ultraviolet rays from the Sun do not make it glow.

UNIT 07
GARDEN HOSE SCIENCE

PRESSURE IS DEFINED AS THE AMOUNT OF FORCE EXERTED OVER A DEFINED AREA. If you try to walk across fresh snow in boots, you'll sink as your weight compresses the snow under your feet. Wearing snowshoes spreads the force of your weight over a larger area, decreasing the pressure you put on the snow and allowing you to walk across the surface like a snowshoe hare.

We live beneath a mass of air that puts constant atmospheric pressure on our bodies and everything surrounding us. If you dive underwater, you add the weight of the water above you to the total pressure you experience.

In this chapter, you'll learn to do a fun water-pressure experiment by elevating a column of water in a hose high enough to lift you up on a water-filled hot-water bottle or an air mattress.

While you have the hose out, fill up a container and explore buoyancy by engineering foil boats. Make some waves, while you're at it, and try your hand at starting a siphon to cool off on a hot summer day.

SIPHON ROLLER COASTER

MATERIALS

→ Water balloons

→ 2 large plastic containers, one of them clear

→ ½ inch to ¾ inch (1.5 to 2 cm) clear, flexible plastic tubing, 6 to 8 feet (1.8 to 2.4 m) long

→ Water

SAFETY TIPS & HINTS

— Never leave young children unattended near water.

— The upper end of the tube must remain submerged at all times, or the siphon won't work.

— This is a good experiment for two or more people.

— Balloon fragments pose a chocking hazard to young children.

SEND BALLOON FRAGMENTS ON A WATERY RIDE THROUGH LOOPS OF PLASTIC TUBING.

Fig. 4: When the siphon is running, feed the balloon fragments into the upper end of the tubing.

PROTOCOL

STEP 1: Have a water balloon fight. Collect and keep fragments of the water balloons. (Fig. 1, 2)

STEP 2: Place a large, clear container on a ledge or chair and use a garden hose to fill it with water. Place the other container next to it, at ground level. (Fig. 3)

STEP 3: Submerge the plastic tubing completely in the water in the upper container so that all air is removed. If there are air bubbles in the tube, move the tubing around underwater until they're all released. You can also use the water coming out of the hose to remove air bubbles from the tubing.

STEP 4: Have someone hold one end of the plastic tubing underwater in the upper container while a second person seals off the other end of the tube with his or her thumb. Have the second person remove the end of the plastic tube from the upper container and move it to the lower container, making sure the covered opening is held lower than the submerged end of the tube.

STEP 5: Continue to hold the upper end of the tube underwater and release water from the lower end of the tube by removing your thumb.

STEP 6: Water should run through the siphon from the upper container into the lower one.

Fig. 1: Have a water balloon fight.

Fig. 2: Pick up the balloon fragments.

Fig. 3: Fill a large container with water.

Fig. 5: Watch the balloon fragments travel through the siphon roller coaster.

STEP 7: Twist and turn the lower end of the tube to create a roller coaster.

STEP 8: Put balloon fragments into the upper end of the tube and watch them travel through the twisted tube. (Fig. 4, 5)

STEP 9: When you're done, pull the upper end of the tube out of the water to stop the siphon.

THE SCIENCE BEHIND THE FUN

Siphons are used for everything from draining swimming pools to irrigating crops since they can move water from one place to another without using a pump.

In a siphon, you have a short column of water going up, over a barrier, and a longer column of water going down. When you release water from the bottom of the tube, pressure and gravity cause the water to move over the barrier and into the lower container.

These forces continue to push water up to the top of the barrier, over the hump, and into the lower tube in a cycle that is broken if air gets into the upper tube.

CREATIVE ENRICHMENT

1. If you straighten out the tubing by putting your upper container on different steps of a step ladder, does the height of the upper container affect how fast balloons travel through the tube, from one end to the other? Use a timer to check.

2. What will happen to the rate of water moving through the siphon if you use a longer piece of tube to make the lower column longer?

KIDDIE POOL BOATS

MATERIALS

→ Large, water-filled container, such as a kiddie pool

→ Three 12 x 12-inch (30.5 x 30.5 cm) sheets of aluminum foil, plus more for additional boats

→ Coins

SAFETY TIPS & HINTS

— Never leave young children unattended near water.

— Coins present a choking hazard to young children.

MAKE FOIL BOATS TO TEST HOW SHAPE AFFECTS FLOTATION.

Fig. 4: Design more boats and test them in the water.

PROTOCOL

STEP 1: Fill a container with water. Put a piece of aluminum foil in the water, edge first. Watch what happens.

STEP 2: Crumple up the piece of aluminum foil. Drop it in the water to see whether it floats or sinks. (Fig. 1)

STEP 3: Form another piece of foil into a boat to see whether it will float. (Fig. 2)

Fig. 1: Crumple up a piece of aluminum foil to see whether it floats or sinks.

Fig. 2: Form a piece of foil into a boat.

STEP 4: See how many pennies you can add to the boat before it sinks. (Fig. 3)

STEP 5: Redesign your boat with another piece of foil to see whether you can get more coins in before it sinks. (Fig. 4)

Fig. 3: Add coins to the boat.

CREATIVE ENRICHMENT

1. Test the buoyancy of some other materials, such as wood, plastic, rock, and metal.

2. In a big swimming pool, what shapes can you make with your body to help you sink or stay afloat?

3. Compare what happens when you put a water balloon in the pool versus an air-filled balloon the same size. What happens if you fill a balloon with half water, half air?

THE SCIENCE BEHIND THE FUN

Buoyancy is the ability to float. To make something float that would normally sink, you have to change its shape so that it displaces, or pushes out of the way, at least its own weight in water.

Increasing how much space something takes up, which is called *volume*, decreases its average density, which is loosely defined as weight divided by volume. To float, boats have to be designed in shapes that will displace at least as much water as they weigh. For example, a 100-pound (45.3 kg) block of metal won't move much water out of the way and will sink quickly, but a 100-pound (45.3 kg) block of metal reshaped into a boat pushes much more water out of the way and will float.

A flat sheet of foil is denser than water and sinks if you put it in edge first; but when you shape it into a boat, it pushes more water out of the way and can float. Adding coins to the foil boat increases the weight of the boat, and when it gets too heavy, it sinks.

Did your crumpled foil sink? Crumpling up foil traps air inside the foil ball and makes it buoyant. Life jackets work in a similar way and keep you afloat in water because they contain a lot of trapped air.

WAVY SCIENCE

MATERIALS

→ Large container, such as a kiddie pool

→ Water

→ Rocks

→ 2 flat, sturdy objects, such as plasticware lids or cutting boards

→ Long, flexible rope

SAFETY TIPS & HINTS

— Never leave young children unattended near water.

USE WATER AND A ROPE TO OBSERVE ENERGY DISTURBANCES MOVING THROUGH MATTER.

Fig. 1: Drop a rock in the water and observe the wave pattern it makes.

PROTOCOL

STEP 1: Fill the kiddie pool with water.

STEP 2: Drop or toss a rock gently into the middle of the water and observe the wave patterns it makes. Now, drop 2 rocks at the same time in opposite sides of the pool to see what happens. (Fig. 1)

STEP 3: Use a flat object to make a wave by placing it in the water and pushing forward. Change the depth and angle of the object to see how it changes the waves it creates.

STEP 4: With two people, start simultaneous, similar waves from opposite sides of the pool to see what happens when they meet in the middle. (Fig. 2)

Fig. 2: See what happens when two waves meet.

Fig. 3: Make a wave travel through a rope.

STEP 5: Have two people stretch out a rope between them and lay it flat on the ground.

STEP 6: Pick up one end of the rope and rapidly move it up and down to make waves. Try making fast waves and slow waves. Make big waves and small waves. (Fig. 3, 4)

STEP 7: Make similar waves from each end at the same time to see what happens when the waves meet. See page 141 for a link to a video we made of our own waves!

STEP 8: Jump rope, just for fun.

Fig. 4: Make lots of waves.

THE SCIENCE BEHIND THE FUN

We can observe waves many places in the natural world. Waves are disturbances caused by energy moving through mediums such as water, a rope, the air, or even the earth. Vibrations often produce waves, and soundwaves are produced by pressure vibrations in the air.

The jump rope you flick up and down carries energy from one end to the opposite end in waves, but following the passage of a wave, the rope returns to its original spot on the ground. When you drop a stone in the water, the energy of the stone hitting the water creates waves, but the water doesn't move in the direction of the wave.

A wave's crest is its highest point, and its trough is its lowest point. The distance from one crest to another in a wave pattern is called *wavelength*. In this experiment, you see what happens when two waves meet. This is called *interference*.

CREATIVE ENRICHMENT

1. Hold the rope about waist high between two people and try to set up a standing wave pattern by shaking it up and down from one end. See how changing how fast you shake it changes the pattern.

2. Make a kazoo from a comb and a piece of folded tissue paper to hear sound waves produced by vibrations.

WATER ELEVATOR

MATERIALS

→ Duct tape

→ 2 garden hoses

→ Hot water bottle or air mattress

→ Stepladder

→ Funnel whose end fits in the mouth of the hose

→ Rigid, flat object, such as a thick cutting board

SAFETY TIPS & HINTS

— Always use a spotter when standing on a ladder. Young children must be supervised.

— You will need a lot of duct tape for this experiment, to prevent leaks between the hose and the mattress or hot water bottle.

— Remove all air seals from the mouth of the air mattress, so that the water can back up into the hose.

FEEL THE POWER OF WATER PRESSURE IN THIS UPLIFTING EXPERIMENT.

Fig. 1: Turn on the faucet to start the experiment.

PROTOCOL

STEP 1: Duct tape the end of one hose securely to the mouth of a hot water bottle or air mattress so that it won't leak. Use plenty of tape!

STEP 2: Hook up the other hose to a faucet and attach the free end to the top of a stepladder with duct tape.

STEP 3: Raise the free end of the hose attached to the mattress up the ladder, put a funnel in it, and position it so that water will run from the upper hose into the funnel. Attach it in position using duct tape.

Fig. 2: Stand on a cutting board on top of a hot water bottle as it fills.

Fig. 3: An air mattress will take longer to fill, so relax.

STEP 4: Fix leaks and make adjustments. Start the experiment by turning the faucet on and letting it run to fill your bottle or mattress. (Fig. 1)

STEP 5: If using a hot water bottle, put the cutting board on top and stand on it as the bottle fills. It should lift you up. Turn the hose off when the funnel starts to overflow. (Fig. 2)

STEP 6: If using an air mattress, be patient because it will take awhile to fill. Lie down on it if you want, and wait for it to lift you off of the ground. (Fig. 3)

STEP 7: How many people can stand on the water-filled air mattress?

CREATIVE ENRICHMENT

Measure the height of the water column you create by measuring the distance from the ground to the funnel. Calculate how much water pressure you are exerting with 1 square foot (30.5 cm²) of water at the bottom of your container.

THE SCIENCE BEHIND THE FUN

When you fill an air mattress using an elevated hose, the water runs into the container until it is full and water rises in the hose. The pressure at the bottom of the water column in the hose is transmitted into the vessel, and a law of physics called *Pascal's Law* says that this fluid pressure is transmitted equally in all directions. As water rises in the hose, the pressure rises in the container.

One cubic foot (0.03 m³) of water weighs 62.4 pounds (28.3 kg) of pressure per square foot (0.1 m²). So if you have 1 cubic foot (0.03 m³) of water sitting in a vessel that is 1 foot (30.5 cm) on each side, it exerts 62.4 pounds (28.3 kg) of pressure on the bottom of the vessel.

If you divide 62.4 pounds (28.3 kg) per square foot by 144 square inches (929 cm²), you get 0.43 pounds (195 g) per square inch (6.5 cm²). The pressure at a depth of 1 foot (30.5 cm) of water is 0.43 pounds (195 g) per square inch (6.5 cm²). So, the height of the water in the hose determines how much pressure is in the mattress or water bottle, which determines how much weight it can hold.

With 6 feet (1.8 m) of water standing in your hose, you're getting about 2.6 pounds (1.2 kg) per square inch (6.5 cm²), so 1 square foot (0.1 m²) is exerting around 372 pounds (168.7 kg) of force. That's a lot of force!

UNIT 8
PLAYGROUND PHYSICS

PLAYGROUNDS ARE LIFE-SIZE PHYSICS EXPERIMENTS. YOU SWING ON PENDULUMS, SLIDE DOWN RAMPS, SEESAW ON GIANT LEVERS, AND SPIN ON CENTRIFUGES.

Before the first modern playground was constructed in England, kids ran around in the streets, sliding and swinging on whatever they could find. Modern playground equipment had yet to be invented, but in 1923, an Englishman named Charles Wicksteed erected the first formal playground swings from factory pipes tied together at the top with chains. They were reportedly dizzyingly high, with no safety net below, and everyone loved them. An advocate of children's recreation, Wicksteed went on to invent more swings and slides and started a playground equipment manufacturing company that still exists today.

What would you invent if someone asked you to engineer a new playground contraption? Think about it the next time you swing, slide, and spin your way across a playground.

RAMP RACES

SEE WHICH KIND OF FOOD ROLLS FASTEST.

MATERIALS

→ 2 cans of equal size and weight, one containing liquid (e.g., tomato sauce), one containing beans

→ Playground slide or homemade ramp

→ Yardstick

→ Phone with camera and stopwatch (optional)

→ Food cans with different diameters, lengths, and weights

→ Toy cars and trucks

SAFETY TIPS & HINTS

— Exercise caution so that rolling cans don't hit kids at the bottom of the slide.

Fig. 1: Race the liquid can against the bean can.

PROTOCOL

STEP 1: Line up the cans at the top of the slide. You can use a yardstick as the starting line to release the cans from the same height.

STEP 2: Guess which can will win the race. Your guess is your hypothesis.

Fig. 2: Race a full can against an empty can.

Fig. 3: Race a big can against a smaller can.

Fig. 4: Race cars down the ramp.

STEP 3: Release the cans at exactly the same time and record which one hits the bottom of the slide first. You can use a phone camera and stopwatch for precise measurements. (Fig. 1)

STEP 4: Create more races with different size cans of different weights. (Fig. 2, 3)

STEP 5: Try racing toy cars down a ramp. Can you predict which one will win? How is this experiment different than racing cans? (Fig. 4)

CREATIVE ENRICHMENT

1. Race two cans of similar weight and contents but with different diameters down the slide.

2. Take a video of a can race with a yardstick near the bottom of the slide.

3. Watch it in slow motion on film-editing software that tells you how many frames per second you are watching and calculate the exact speed of your cans.

THE SCIENCE BEHIND THE FUN

Gravity is the force that pulls you down a slide. All objects, regardless of size or mass, will slide down a frictionless ramp with the same acceleration, but rolling is a different story.

At the top of the slide, your liquid and bean cans have close to the same potential energy because they have very similar weights. This potential energy is converted into kinetic energy (the energy of motion) as they roll. Whichever can is able to convert the most energy into translational kinetic energy (the energy of something moving in a straight line) will roll the fastest.

In the bean can, all the beans stick together, and the entire mass of the can and beans has to spin as it rolls down the ramp. Lots of energy is converted into the energy of rotation.

In a can full of liquid, the majority of liquid doesn't move with the outside of the can, so most of the mass inside the can moves directly down the ramp without spinning at all. The potential energy it had at the top of the slide is converted directly into translational kinetic energy.

That means that the can full of liquid should beat the can full of beans to the bottom of the slide if you release them at the same time.

SWING PENDULUM

MATERIALS

→   Playground swing

SAFETY TIPS & HINTS

— You'll need two people for
this experiment.

— The person swinging
shouldn't pump his or her
legs for the first part of the
experiment, or it won't work.

— If you're timing swing
periods, time ten periods and
then divide by ten to get an
average period time.

EXPLORE SOME OF THE PHYSICAL FORCES AT PLAY WHEN
YOU SWING.

Fig. 4: Can you stay together?

PROTOCOL

STEP 1: Have one person sit on the swing with his or her legs out in front.

STEP 2: Grasp the swing from behind and pull the swing up and back as far as possible. (Fig. 1)

Fig. 1: Pull a person back on a swing.

Fig. 2: When the swing comes back, it won't hit you.

Fig. 3: Try synchronized swinging.

STEP 3: Let go of the swing without pushing it and don't step back. Stand straight up where you released the swing.

STEP 4: The person on the swing will swing back but shouldn't hit you. (Fig. 2)

STEP 5: Try synchronized swinging on swings with the same length chains (stop pumping your legs at the same time) and different chain lengths to see what happens. (Fig. 3, 4)

THE SCIENCE BEHIND THE FUN

Pendulums are weights suspended by strings that move with the help of gravity. They swing back and forth with amazing regularity, and the shorter a pendulum's string, the faster it swings. Playground swings are pendulums, and the time between the release of the swing and when it comes back is called the *period*.

When you walk, you are aided by gravity as your legs swing back and forth like simple pendulums. People with long legs tend to walk with a slower stride than their shorter-legged companions. In this experiment, you'll notice that you swing back and forth more slowly on a long swing than a short one.

A pendulum never swings back past the point at which it was released if no energy is added when you release it. When you pull someone back on a swing and release, he or she won't hit you on the swing back as long as you don't add energy by pushing.

CREATIVE ENRICHMENT

Time the periods for people of different weights and for swings with chains of different lengths to see how the period changes. Does the period depend on how high you swing?

35 PICNIC BLANKET RELATIVITY

MATERIALS

→ Large sheet or picnic blanket

→ Large ball, such as a basketball or soccer ball

→ Smaller balls, such as tennis balls

SAFETY TIPS & HINTS

— This experiment works best with four or more kids.

Fig. 3: What force brings the balls back down?

PROTOCOL

STEP 1: Stand and hold the sheet or blanket as flat and level as possible, parallel to the ground.

STEP 2: Put a large ball in the middle of the blanket. What happens to the blanket? (Fig. 1)

STEP 3: With the large ball still on the blanket, put the smaller balls on the blanket to see what happens.

Fig. 1: Put a ball in the middle of a blanket you're holding flat.

Fig. 2: Toss the balls into the air.

STEP 4: Toss the balls as high into the air as you can and try to catch them on the blanket. What pulls them back down? (Fig. 2, 3)

CREATIVE ENRICHMENT

Try the same experiment on a trampoline, with a person standing in the middle. Do the balls roll toward where the person is standing?

THE SCIENCE BEHIND THE FUN

Albert Einstein was a famous scientist with new ways of thinking about space and time. He visualized them together, as a fabric, sort of like the picnic blanket you suspend in the air for this experiment.

He theorized that massive bodies, such as stars and planets, create warps and curves in the flexible fabric of space and time, in much the same way that a heavy ball bends the fabric of your blanket. This theory is called *general relativity*.

Earth and the other planets that orbit the Sun follow curves in the spatial fabric of our solar system, created by the massive star (the Sun) at its center. You can see how the smaller balls you put on your blanket roll to the area where the larger ball is curving the fabric.

The balls you throw into the air are pulled down by the same force that attracts the Moon to the Earth and the planets to the Sun! We call this force gravity.

UNIT 9
GLORIOUS GARDENING

BARLEY, RICE, WHEAT, PEAS, AND SQUASH WERE SOME OF THE FIRST CROPS THAT HUMANS CULTIVATED IN ANCIENT FIELDS AND GARDENS.
For thousands of years, people have treasured seeds that grow fast, foil pests, and yield tasty food. Long before people started playing with plant DNA in labs, farmers and gardeners were selectively breeding new plant hybrids, cross-pollinating and grafting favorite plant species to perfect their produce.

Today, modern agriculture is experiencing an onslaught of issues. Even with a wealth of science at our fingertips, food safety, crop diversity, and delicate ecosystems are all at risk as we fight to feed an exploding world population. Should an agricultural apocalypse ever befall us, forward thinkers have built seed vaults in places such as the North Pole, sheltering frozen seeds from thousands of plant species.

With water, sunlight, warmth, and nutrient-rich soil, you can grow your own food from seeds. In this chapter, you'll have a race to see how fast seeds sprout, watch seedlings maneuver toward the light, and compost kitchen scraps to make fertilizer.

LAB 36

ALLELOPATHY EXPERIMENT

SPROUT SEEDS TO LEARN HOW SOME PLANTS USE CHEMICAL WARFARE TO DEFEND THEIR SPACE.

MATERIALS

→ 1 large rectangular planter, or several small flowerpots or cups

→ Potting soil

→ Ice pop sticks or wooden garden markers

→ 2 or more of the following: lemons, oranges, black walnuts, pine needles, mint, eucalyptus leaves, chrysanthemum leaves, or tomato plant leaves

→ Mortar and pestle, food processor, or other tool for grinding nuts

→ Citrus zester or grater

→ Chia seeds or radish seeds

Fig. 3: Mix substances into the soil.

SAFETY TIPS & HINTS

— Black walnuts are tree nuts, so be allergy aware.

PROTOCOL

STEP 1: Fill your planting containers with potting soil.

STEP 2: Subdivide large containers with ice pop sticks, with a section for each substance you want to test, plus one section with no substances, as a control. Label each section with an ice pop stick or garden marker. If using small pots, label one for each substance, plus a control.

Fig. 1: Grind black walnuts or crush leaves.

Fig. 2: Grate citrus peels.

STEP 3: Grind nuts, grate citrus peels, and chop or crush leaves to create mixable versions of the substances you want to test, cleaning your tools in between to avoid cross-contamination. (Fig. 1, 2)

STEP 4: Mix each of the substances into the top few inches (7 to 10 cm) of the section or pot you have labeled for them. Don't mix anything into the control section. (Fig. 3)

STEP 5: Plant chia or radish seeds in each section. Make pencil holes to plant the same number of seeds in each section, or put a few teaspoons (13 to 17 g) of seed in each pot or section and mix them evenly into the soil.

STEP 6: Gently water the seeds.

STEP 7: Check the seeds every day. Record when they sprout in each section and which substances appear to have allelopathic effects on seed growth, preventing them from sprouting or growing. (Fig. 4)

Fig. 4: See what substances affect seed growth.

CREATIVE ENRICHMENT

Collect invasive plants such as buckthorn, garlic mustard, spotted knapweed, and nutsedge to test the allelopathic effects of their leaves, seeds, and fruit.

THE SCIENCE BEHIND THE FUN

Plants need their space. Some even make biochemicals that force other plants to back off. This process is called *allelopathy*, which literally means mutual harm. While some of these chemicals are toxic to competitors, others may interfere with cooperative relationships between plants and other organisms. At any rate, preventing new seedlings from popping up nearby gives plants more room to grow.

Invasive species are especially good at producing these allelopathic substances, which may explain how they spread so far and fast when introduced to a new environment.

Since many plants exude these toxins into the soil from their roots and complex ecosystems are involved, it is tricky to design a meaningful experiment to explore this phenomenon. However, it's fun to test the general allelopathic effect of plant compounds on seed germination with this project.

LAB 37

COMPREHENDING COMPOST

MATERIALS

→ Biodegradable kitchen waste such as coffee grounds, fruit and vegetable scraps, and egg shells

→ 2 containers, such as buckets or cups

→ 2 small pieces of plastic, such as milk container lids

→ Shovel

→ Soil thermometer or instant-read thermometer for meat

SAFETY TIPS & HINTS

— Always call your local electric company before you dig to avoid underground power lines.

— This experiment will work best during months when it is warm outside.

DIG A HOLE IN THE DIRT TO LEARN MORE ABOUT THE NUTRIENT CYCLE AND MAKE FERTILIZER FOR YOUR GARDEN.

Fig. 3: Dump compost in the holes.

PROTOCOL

STEP 1: Save some compostable waste from your kitchen. Divide the compost equally into two containers. Add a small piece of plastic to each container so you can observe what happens to plastic in compost heaps and landfills. (Fig. 1)

Fig. 1: Save some compostable waste from your kitchen.

Fig. 2: Dig two holes in the ground.

STEP 2: Dig two holes in the ground. They should each be about 1 foot (30.5 cm) deep. (Fig. 2)

STEP 3: Empty one compost container into each hole and cover them with dirt. (Fig. 3)

STEP 4: Label one compost pile "no water" and the other "water."

STEP 5: Water the compost pile labeled "water" every other day or so.

STEP 6: When you water the compost, use a soil thermometer or another metal thermometer to check the temperature in each of your compost piles. Record it and compare it to the soil temperature in the surrounding areas. (Fig. 4)

STEP 7: After several weeks, dig up your compost to observe how well things are breaking down. Spread it out on a tarp or plastic bag to get a closer look.

STEP 8: Put the compost back in the ground and add it to your garden as fertilizer when it is ready. Recycle the pieces of plastic.

Fig. 4: Check the temperature of the compost.

CREATIVE ENRICHMENT

1. Test how packing down compost to limit oxygen or adding grass clippings and leaves affects compost.

2. Record how many worms you find in and near your compost piles.

THE SCIENCE BEHIND THE FUN

In ecosystems everywhere, nutrients move from one generation to the next. Primary producers such as plants take them up from the soil and air. Plants are then eaten by animals that may be eaten by other animals. Eventually, plants and animals die and decompose, freeing up nutrients to be taken up once more by primary producers, rebooting the cycle.

Decomposers such as bacteria and fungi eat dead things, breaking them down to use as energy. In a damp, healthy compost pile, decomposers grow quickly, producing enough heat to kill pests and even some harmful bacteria. Decomposers need water to grow happily and some need oxygen to break down food more efficiently, which is why compost should occasionally be mixed with a shovel.

You can build or buy a larger compost system to break down all of your compostable waste and make nutrient-rich fertilizer for your garden.

LAB 38 — PLANT RACE

MATERIALS

→ 1 large planter, or several small flowerpots or cups

→ Potting soil

→ Ice pope sticks or wooden plant markers

→ A variety of seeds and dry beans

SAFETY TIPS & HINTS

— Be aware that dry beans can be choking hazards for small children.

CREATE A BOTANICAL OLYMPICS TO SEE HOW QUICKLY DIFFERENT PLANTS GROW.

Fig. 4: See which plants grow the fastest.

PROTOCOL

STEP 1: Fill the containers with potting soil.

STEP 2: Subdivide large containers with sticks, with a section for each type of plant in the race.

STEP 3: Label each pot or section according to which seeds you will plant there. (Fig. 1)

STEP 4: Plant seeds or beans in each pot or section according to directions on the package. (Fig. 2)

Fig. 1: Divide and label planting containers.

Fig. 2: Plant seeds or beans according to directions.

STEP 5: Water the seeds you planted. (Fig. 3)

STEP 6: In your science notebook, make a guess, or hypothesis, about which plants you think will grow the fastest and why.

STEP 7: Observe the plants for a few weeks. Once they've sprouted, record in your notebook how tall they are each day and when leaves form. (Fig. 4)

STEP 8: Check to see whether your experimental results agree with your hypothesis.

Fig. 3: Water the seeds.

THE SCIENCE BEHIND THE FUN

Plants that grow very quickly may have an advantage over their neighbors, as they lay claim to nutrients, space, and light. Some bamboos, for example, can grow several inches (15 to 20 cm) a day, as they shoot up, competing for sunlight. It's interesting to observe different plant species to see whether they start off growing very fast and then slow down or continue to grow rapidly.

To grow, seeds imbibe, or drink, water to free up nutrients and enzymes they need for energy, and the first thing to emerge from their seed coat is a tiny root. A sprout soon follows, growing toward the light. Once in the light, a plant will turn green and produce leaves.

How do you think the results of this experiment would differ if you did your plant race in the dark? Try it!

CREATIVE ENRICHMENT

1. Graph your results to make a growth curve for each type of seed. Do they start fast and slow down or continue to grow at the same rate?

2. Race the same type of seeds against each other, but water them with different liquids. Use tap water as a control.

3. See how density affects growth rate by racing seeds grown very close together against seeds grown far from one another.

LAB 39 · GARDEN GUEST BOOK

MATERIALS

→ Notebook

→ Garden

→ Magnifying glass

→ Camera (optional)

→ Flashlight

SAFETY TIPS & HINTS

— Visit the garden at different times of day and night.

PROTOCOL

STEP 1: Start a garden guest book section in your science notebook for garden visitors. (Fig. 1)

STEP 2: Observe flower and vegetable gardens to find out what creatures are visiting. See what's under leaves and crawling in the dirt, as well as who is sitting on plants and flying through the air. Use your magnifying glass for a closer look. (Fig. 2, 3)

STEP 3: Use your garden guest book to record, draw, and insert photos of the creatures you observe. Keep track of the day and time you saw the visitors, which plants they were on or near, and what they appeared to be doing. (Fig. 4)

STEP 4: Try to identify the animals, birds, insects, and arthropods you observed.

Fig. 1: Start a garden guest book.

STEP 5: Visit the same garden or gardens over several days at different times of day to see what you find. Observe gardens at night, with a flashlight, to discover nocturnal visitors.

Fig. 2: Look for spiders.

Fig. 3: Keep an eye out for toads.

Fig. 4: Draw and describe the garden visitors you spot.

CREATIVE ENRICHMENT

Did you find predators, for example, spiders? Make a garden guest food chain diagram that includes the plants in the garden. Where do you fit in?

THE SCIENCE BEHIND THE FUN

Although gardeners sometimes apply herbicides and insecticides to kill weeds and bugs, certain chemicals can be harmful to the environment and other animals. It's much more fun to skip the sprays, pull garden weeds by hand, and see what creatures visit the diverse ecosystem of a garden. In a healthy, species-rich plot, even pests such as aphids can be controlled by natural predators, such as ladybugs and tiny wasps.

Keeping a garden guest book will give you a glimpse into another world and help you see how each creature is part of a larger puzzle. From worms in the dirt to insects and birds, every living thing occupies a niche, playing a role in the small ecosystem of a garden and the larger ecosystem of our planet.

UNIT 10
EXCELLENT ECOLOGY

THE WORD *ECOSYSTEM* DESCRIBES THE INEXORABLY INTERTWINED RELATIONSHIPS AMONG LIVING ORGANISMS, THEIR PHYSICAL ENVIRONMENTS, AND ALL OF THE OTHER ORGANISMS SHARING THE SAME SPACE. While some ecosystems are small, such as a decaying tree trunk, each ecosystem is part of a larger one, for instance, an island, a rainforest, or even an entire planet.

All living things depend on healthy ecosystems for survival. Here on Earth, there are a limited number of resources, and what happens in one ecosystem often impacts others, sometimes reaching all the way across the globe.

Currently, the world is losing species at an unusually high rate, largely as a result of human behavior. Scientists who study our planet, the environment, and creatures that live here are trying to understand what we can do to best protect the delicate balance of Earth's larger ecosystem, which sustains us all.

The labs in this unit will help you get a closer look at the ecosystems that surround you. You'll be amazed by the diversity of life in your own backyard.

LAB 40

PROTECTED PITFALL TRAPS

MATERIALS

→ Garden trowel

→ Collection container such as a cup, bucket, can, or plastic container

→ Plastic lid slightly larger than the container (optional)

→ Rocks to elevate the lid (optional)

→ White cloth

→ Magnifying glass

SAFETY TIPS & HINTS

— Don't set traps where people are likely to step in them.

— You'll probably catch more insects in shady spots than sunny ones.

— Don't pick up insects with bare hands unless you know they don't bite or sting.

CREATE HIDDEN TRAPS TO CAPTURE CREEPING CREATURES.

Fig. 3: See what falls in the trap.

PROTOCOL

STEP 1: Select a spot for your pitfall trap. Gardens and areas near trees and plants are good places to sample arthropod populations.

Fig. 1: Dig a hole for your container.

Fig. 2: Cover the trap with a raised lid.

STEP 2: Use a trowel to dig a hole a little deeper than your collection container. (Fig. 1)

STEP 3: Place the collection container in the hole and fill dirt around it so that the top of the container is flush with the surrounding soil.

STEP 4: Camouflage the edges of the container with leaves, if you want.

STEP 5: For a protected trap, set rocks around the edges of the container and place a lid on top to make an elevated roof for your trap. This will protect whatever falls into the pit from drowning if it rains. (Fig. 2)

STEP 6: Check your trap daily to see what falls in. Gently shake what you catch onto a white cloth or towel. (Fig. 3)

STEP 7: Observe each arthropod with a magnifying glass. Record its approximate size and draw it in your science notebook. Set the arthropods free where you caught them. (Fig. 4)

STEP 8: Try to identify the arthropods you captured in your pitfall trap.

Fig. 4: Observe the creatures you catch.

CREATIVE ENRICHMENT

Set pit traps in a wooded area, an area with tall grass, weeds, and wildflowers, and a manicured grass lawn to compare how the arthropods you catch differ.

THE SCIENCE BEHIND THE FUN

Insects, arachnids, and other arthropods play a crucial role in Earth's ecosystems. Some are helpful to humans, such as pollinating honeybees, while others are harmful, for example, Lyme disease–carrying ticks. It's helpful to understand how insect populations shrink and grow so that we can support helpful arthropods and control harmful ones. Because arthropods serve as food for larger animals, the insect population in an area can have a noticeable effect on bird and bat populations.

Ecologists use pitfall traps to study ground-dwelling arthropod populations. With global temperatures rising, many arthropods are moving north, and people are seeing species they've never encountered before. In this experiment, you can observe some of the insect populations in your own backyard. If you enjoy this lab, find a citizen science project that lets you help scientists monitor insect populations in your area (see *Resources* on page 141).

LAB 41 — ALGAE AQUARIUM

DO SOME WATER TESTING TO SEE WHERE ALGAE THRIVE.

MATERIALS

→ Clear jars or bowls

→ Bottled spring water or tap water left to sit overnight to remove chlorine

→ Small cups for taking samples

→ 1/8 teaspoon sugar, for each sample

→ Microscope (optional)

SAFETY TIPS & HINTS

— Never leave young children unattended near water.

Fig. 3: Take more water samples.

PROTOCOL

STEP 1: Fill several jars or bowls halfway with chlorine-free water. (Fig. 1)

STEP 2: Think of places algae might grow, such as lakes, streams, puddles, and pools. You can also test other natural objects, such as plants. Label each jar and bottle with a sample name.

Fig. 1: Pour the chlorine-free water into jars.

Fig. 2: Take water samples.

STEP 3: Take small samples of water or objects from the areas you chose and add them to the jars of water. Add sugar to each of the jars to speed the growth of algae. (Fig. 2, 3)

STEP 4: Loosely cover or leave the lids off the jars and let them sit in a covered area for several weeks, checking for algae growth. Add more bottled water if they start to dry out. Record algae growth and the color of the algae from the different sources. (Fig. 4)

STEP 5: If you have a microscope, look at the algae under magnification.

Fig. 4: See where algae grows.

THE SCIENCE BEHIND THE FUN

Algae may seem like your foe, if you've ever planned to swim in a lake that's turned green overnight. If you live by the sea, you may have heard that some marine algae blooms produce "red tides," which contain deadly toxins. Recently, algae blooms have become problematic, as too many agricultural chemicals make their way into lakes and streams.

On a brighter note, this microscopic plant that lacks a stem, root, and leaves is also being heralded as a possible producer of alternative energy.

But that's just the human perspective. Food chains illustrate why algae are so important by showing us how energy moves around in Earth's ecosystem. Primary producers, such as plants and algae, use the Sun's energy to make carbohydrates and oxygen from carbon dioxide and water. These primary producers are eaten by consumers, such as fish, which in turn are eaten by other consumers, for example, bears, as energy is passed from organism to organism. Without the food and oxygen from primary producers, we wouldn't be here.

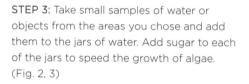

CREATIVE ENRICHMENT

Many metals hinder the growth of algae and other microscopic organisms. Create your own experiment, using one of your algae cultures to test different metals (e.g., coins) to see whether they slow the growth of the algae. Be sure to have a control sample and record everything in your science notebook.

42 CAPTURE-MARK-RECAPTURE

MATERIALS

→ Tape measure

→ Sticks or garden markers

→ String

→ Container for bugs, such as an empty plastic container

→ Science notebook

→ White correction ink or white nail polish

SAFETY TIPS & HINTS

— In areas with poisonous snakes, use caution when lifting rocks and logs.

— You can usually find isopods under rocks, mulch, small logs, and paving stones.

Fig. 3: Mark isopods with white ink or nail polish.

CATCH AND TAG ISOPODS SUCH AS PILL BUGS TO STUDY THEIR POPULATION SIZE.

PROTOCOL

STEP 1: Hunt for an area containing isopods, such as pill bugs and sow bugs. Look under rocks and logs. (Fig. 1)

STEP 2: Measure and mark off the area you want to sample using a tape measure, sticks, and string. For example, mark off a square area that is 6½ feet (2 m) on each side.

STEP 3: Lift up a rock or log inside the area, collect any isopods you see, put them in a container, and count them. Record the total number of isopods in your notebook. (Fig. 2)

STEP 4: Gently mark each isopod with white correction ink or nail polish. (Fig. 3)

Fig. 1: Hunt for an area with isopods under rocks and logs.

Fig. 2: Lift up rocks to find isopods.

STEP 5: Return the rock or log to its original position and release the isopods nearby. Leave your marked-off square standing.

STEP 6: After a few days, resample the same area, recording the total number of isopods you find and how many of them are marked with white. (Fig. 4)

STEP 7: Divide the number of marked isopods you recaptured on your second visit by the total number of isopods you found that day. Then, divide the number of isopods you marked the first day by that result. This will tell you approximately how many isopods live in the area you tested.

Fig. 4: After a few days, resample the same area to see how many marked isopods you find.

THE SCIENCE BEHIND THE FUN

From collaring bears to tagging snails, scientists use the capture-mark-recapture method to study animal populations. It's an especially helpful method to use when it's not practical to capture and count every single animal in a large area, such as a national park.

In this lab, by capturing and recapturing isopods in a defined area, you can estimate population size by dividing the total number of bugs you marked the first day by the percentage of bugs you find marked on your second visit.

If you capture and mark ten isopods in 1 square meter (10.8 ft²) area of your backyard, release them, come back in a week, and find that two of the ten bugs you capture are marked (20 percent), you would divide ten by 0.2 and estimate that there are about fifty isopods in that area.

CREATIVE ENRICHMENT

Design a capture-mark-recapture experiment for a national park, including details about the population you want to study, how you will tag or label the animals, how long you will wait to recapture them, and how the information you glean could be used.

MOONLIT NATURE WALK

MATERIALS

→ Guide to local wildlife and star map

→ Insect repellent

→ Comfortable shoes

→ Thermometer or phone with weather app for telling temperature (optional)

SAFETY TIPS & HINTS

— Walk in a group and dress for the weather.

— Take your walk on a night when the Moon is full or almost full so you can see.

— Set out around twilight.

— Bring flashlights, but keep them off unless you need them. Your eyes will adjust.

— Hike in an area you know well and stay on the path or go with a guide at a local nature center.

LET YOUR NIGHT VISION KICK IN ON A NOCTURNAL ADVENTURE.

Fig. 4: Take a nature walk on a night when the Moon is full.

PROTOCOL

STEP 1: Will you be walking in a prairie, at the seashore, or in a forest? Is it summer or winter? Research which animals you might see and hear at night. Look at a star map or a star app to find out what constellations you might spy.

Fig. 1: Hit the trail as the sun goes down.

Fig. 2: Your eyes will adjust to the dark.

STEP 2: Put on bug spray and comfortable shoes, and hit the trail when the sun goes down. (Fig. 1)

STEP 3: Walk quietly, stopping frequently to listen. It can take half an hour for your eyes to completely adjust to the dark. Do night sounds change as it gets darker? (Fig. 2)

STEP 4: In summer, listen for crickets. Count how many chirps you hear in fourteen seconds and add forty to get the temperature in Fahrenheit. To calculate the temperature in Celsius, count the chirps in twenty-five seconds, divide by three, and add four. Compare your number to the temperature on your thermometer or phone. It should be pretty close! (Fig. 3)

STEP 5: Close your eyes and breathe in. Does the air smell different at night? (Fig. 4)

STEP 6: Look at the stars. Can you find the Big Dipper or the Milky Way?

STEP 7: Listen for frogs and see how many different calls you hear.

Fig. 3: Close your eyes and listen.

CREATIVE ENRICHMENT

Bring a UV/black light flashlight on your night walk to look for fluorescent fungi and fauna, including certain lichens, scorpions, and millipedes that will glow under the beam.

THE SCIENCE BEHIND THE FUN

The world changes at night. Even as retinal cells in your eyes undergo night-vision-inducing chemical changes, song birds fall silent, hidden creatures emerge, and a nocturnal choir bursts into song. Our well-developed but often underutilized senses of hearing, smell, and even touch are heightened in dim light.

Besides being musicians, crickets are cold-blooded thermometers that take on the temperature of their surroundings. This has an effect on how quickly chemical reactions can occur inside their bodies, which in turn affects how fast they can chirp. Only male crickets make this sound, to attract mates and tell other males to stay away. They chirp by rubbing the sawlike edge of one wing against their other wing and usually stop fiddling once the temperature drops below 55°F (13°C).

QUADRAT SAMPLING

→ 4 stakes or ice pop sticks

→ Measuring tape

→ About 16 feet (5 m) of string or yarn

→ Science notebook

→ Plant identification book or app

SAFETY TIPS & HINTS

— Avoid placing your quadrat where there is poison ivy or poison oak.

— Bring extra stakes along, in case some break.

EMBARK ON AN ECOLOGICAL STAKEOUT TO OBSERVE PLANTS.

Fig. 4: Mark off about 3 feet (1 m) with string.

PROTOCOL

STEP 1: Choose the area you want to sample. A lightly wooded area works well for amateur ecologists.

STEP 2: Place a stake or ice pop stick in the ground at a random spot.

STEP 3: Measure a spot about 3 feet (1 m) away from the stake and place another stake in the ground. (Fig. 1)

STEP 4: Tie your string between the two stakes.

STEP 5: Place another stake about 3 feet (1 m) away from each of the first two stakes to form a square. (Fig. 2)

STEP 6: Use the string to connect the stakes, marking off an area of about 3 feet (1 m). This is called a *quadrat*. (Fig. 3, 4)

STEP 7: Count the total number of trees and plants inside the square and record the number in your notebook.

Fig. 1: Measure out a grid.

Fig. 2. Place stakes at the corners.

Fig. 3: Tie strings between stakes.

THE SCIENCE BEHIND THE FUN

Quadrat sampling is used by scientists to get an idea of how many plants or animals inhabit a certain area and the number of each species living there. Many scientists use inflexible wood or metal grids for this type of sampling, but flexible grids like the one you use in this lab are better for studying areas with trees.

How you design an ecological sampling experiment such as this one depends on what you want to learn. For example, if you're studying giant redwood tree populations, you will need a much larger grid than someone studying the distribution of moss species.

STEP 8: Try to identify the trees and plants contained in the square and how many there are of each species you find.

STEP 9: Remove the stakes and string, walk several feet (2 to 2.5 m) in a random direction, and repeat steps 2 through 8.

STEP 10: After taking at least two quadrat samples, compare your results. Are the number of plants and species consistent in each grid?

CREATIVE ENRICHMENT

1. Design and build a rigid quadrat using wood or metal.

2. Calculate species density for each type of plant or tree you found in this lab.

3. Figure out approximately how many quadrats it would take to cover the entire ecosystem you are sampling.

UNIT 11
EARTH SCIENCE

CAVES ARE UNDERGROUND PASSAGES AND CAVERNS CARVED BY WATER AND LAVA. In their relatively undisturbed interiors, dripping water and volcanic activity deposit minerals that can form stalactites, stalagmites, and crystals.

Mexico's unearthly Cave of Crystals looks like the inside of a geode. The hot, crystallized cavern lies deep underground, near a magma chamber, and some of its transparent crystals are more than 35 feet (11 m) long.

Troglobites, troglophytes, and trogloxenes are creatures who hang out in caves. While troglobites such as blind fish must spend their entire lives in caves, troglophytes are able to creep out of their subterranean dwellings. Trogloxenes such as bats pass time in caves but depend on the outside world as well. Cave ecosystems are unusual in that most caves are devoid of sunlight, making energy scarce and limiting resources.

This Earth Science unit includes labs that show you how to replicate crystal formation in caves using baking soda and how to freeze some supercool ice formations.

SUPERCOOL EXPERIMENT

MATERIALS

→ Tap water

→ Large bucket or cooler filled with ice

→ Rock salt, sea salt, or table salt

→ Several 8- or 16-ounce (235 or 475 ml) bottles of purified or distilled bottled water

→ Bowl or plate

SAFETY TIPS & HINTS

— Loosen the lids on the bottles and retighten gently, so they're easy to get off.

— Water for this experiment can be chilled in the freezer.

— Once the water has frozen in a bottle, you must thaw it completely before refreezing it.

— This experiment may take several tries, so don't get frustrated!

Fig. 4: Pour supercooled water slowly over ice.

PUSH THE LIMITS OF FREEZING IN THIS SUPERCHILL EXPERIMENT.

PROTOCOL

STEP 1: Add enough water to your bucket or cooler to come almost to the top of the ice.

STEP 2: Add about ¼ cup (68 g) salt for every 4 gallons (15 L) of ice-water mixture. If you're not sure how much your container holds, measure the ice and water as you add it. Remember, there are 16 cups in every gallon (3.8 L). (Fig. 1)

STEP 3: Empty one or two bottles of water, label them "tap water," and fill them with tap water. Replace the lids.

STEP 4: Set several of your bottles in the ice-water mixture so that their lids are above the ice. Make sure you include at least one tap-water bottle and one purified- or distilled-water bottle. (Fig. 2)

STEP 5: Chill the bottles, checking them frequently, until the water in one of the bottles freezes solid but the water in the other bottles remains liquid. It may take a few hours. (Fig. 3)

STEP 6: Place a few clean ice cubes in a bowl or on a plate.

STEP 7: Carefully remove one of the liquid-water bottles from the ice and gently remove the lid. If it freezes, get another bottle.

Fig. 1: Add ice and salt to a container.

Fig. 2: Put bottles in the ice water to cool.

STEP 8: Once you've found a bottle that doesn't freeze when opened, very slowly pour the water over the ice cubes. If it's supercooled, it will freeze instantly, piling up in a slushy column. (Fig. 4)

STEP 9: If it doesn't work, let your liquid water cool a little bit longer and try again!

STEP 10: See page 141 for a link to a video we took of this supercool experiment!

Fig. 3: Check the bottles frequently for signs of freezing.

CREATIVE ENRICHMENT

Try this experiment with other liquids. Does it work with carbonated beverages?

THE SCIENCE BEHIND THE FUN

Water usually freezes when you cool it below 0°C (32°F), but without a trigger for crystal formation, it is possible for water molecules to remain in a liquid state well below 0°C (32°F). In this experiment, the tap water usually freezes first because ice crystals form on impurities. Crystals can also form on imperfections inside a container. Once a crystal forms, or the water comes into contact with a crystal from another source, the water molecules quickly move into formation around the seed crystal, and the water freezes.

In supercooled water, a lattice of ice crystals can also form as the result of motion or impact. Once crystal formation begins at a single spot, all of the other supercooled water molecules snap into formation, forming solid ice.

CRYSTAL CAVES

MATERIALS

→ Rectangular plastic container (with lid) large enough to hold 2 jars

→ Aluminum foil

→ 2 jars

→ Hot tap water

→ Baking soda

→ Food coloring

→ White paper towel or napkin

→ Spoon or scoop

SAFETY TIPS & HINTS

— It may take a few weeks for the crystal stalactites and stalagmites to grow. Be patient.

— This experiment won't work as well if it's very humid.

— If it's going to rain, use the container lid to protect your crystal cave.

GROW BAKING SODA STALAGMITES AND STALACTITES.

Fig. 5: Crystals may grow around the lip of the jar as well.

PROTOCOL

STEP 1: Create a cave by covering a plastic container with aluminum foil and turning it on its side.

STEP 2: Fill both jars with hot tap water.

STEP 3: Add several spoonfuls of baking soda to each jar until no more will dissolve and there is a layer of baking soda sitting at the bottom of the jar.

STEP 4: Add a few drops of food coloring to each jar, stir, and put the uncovered jars into the cave you made. (Fig. 1, 2)

STEP 5: Cut two long strips of paper towel about ½ inch (1.5 cm) wide. Make a fold in the center of each strip.

STEP 6: Position the paper strips with their ends in the jars to form two bridges, with a low-hanging fold in the center. Be sure the ends of each bridge are submerged in liquid.

STEP 7: Wait a few minutes and check to make sure that liquid is moving from each side to the middle of the paper bridge. It will probably drip. (Fig. 3)

STEP 8: Leave your cave in a sheltered area so the baking soda solution can continue to drip. Check it every day or two. If the paper dries out, spoon some liquid from each jar onto the paper to restart the dripping.

STEP 9: After several days, you should see stalactites (downward-growing crystals) and stalagmites (upward-growing crystal) forming in your cave. (Fig. 4, 5)

Fig. 1: Add food coloring to the baking soda and water solution.

Fig. 2: Put the jars into the caves you made.

Fig. 3: Liquid will drip from the paper bridge between the jars.

Fig. 4: You will see stalactites and stalagmites forming in the cave you made.

CREATIVE ENRICHMENT

Try using other solutions, such as one made from Epsom salts and water, to form crystals in your cave.

THE SCIENCE BEHIND THE FUN

In caves, *stalactites* form as the result of water dripping down from the ceiling, carrying along minerals that build up over time to form hanging icicle-like structures. Below the dripping stalactites, minerals may accumulate in piles that reach up toward the ceiling and are called *stalagmites*. Many of these subterranean wonders take thousands of years to form. This lab lets you grow cavelike crystals in a few days or a few weeks.

Surface tension and capillary action pull water and dissolved baking soda up the paper, over the lip of the jar, and down to the lowest point of the bridge, where it collects and drips. Some of the water evaporates, leaving baking soda crystals behind. Over time, you should find crystals growing both up and down, just as you would in a real cave.

SOIL FILTRATION

MATERIALS

→ At least 2 empty 2-liter (2 qt) bottles

→ Jars

→ Rocks slightly larger than the mouth of the bottles

→ Sand

→ Topsoil

→ Liquid cup measure

→ Tap water

→ Science notebook

→ Pitcher of water tinted purple with red and blue food coloring

→ Grass or peat moss

→ Pebbles

SAFETY TIPS & HINTS

— Don't be frustrated if the water is very cloudy or dirty after the first step. You may have to run several rounds of water through the filters to start to see a difference, depending on the type of sand and soil you are testing.

— Do not drink the water you collect from the filter.

"POLLUTE" WATER WITH FOOD COLORING AND TRY TO CLEAN IT UP WITH THE HELP OF NATURAL SOIL FILTERS.

Fig. 4: Pour colored water over the filters.

PROTOCOL

STEP 1: Cut the bottoms off the plastic bottles.

STEP 2: Place the bottles mouth side down into the jars.

STEP 3: Put a layer of rocks in the bottom of each bottle. (Fig. 1)

Fig. 1: Add rocks to the bottom of each bottle.

Fig. 2: Add sand to one of the bottles.

STEP 4: To one bottle, add a deep layer of sand on top of the rocks. (Fig. 2)

STEP 5: To a second bottle, add a deep layer of topsoil on top of the rocks.

STEP 6: Guess which filter will work best and then pour 1 cup (235 ml) of clear tap water over each filter to test your hypothesis. Observe and record the filtered water's appearance in your notebook. (Fig. 3)

STEP 7: Discard the water from the jars.

STEP 8: Pour 1 cup (235 ml) of purple water over each filter (the food coloring is your fake pollutant), observe the filtrate, and record the results.

STEP 9: Continue to layer materials, such as grass or peat moss and pebbles, onto the filters to see what other natural materials aid in water filtration.

STEP 10: Test your filters by pouring equal volumes of colored water over them to observe the color and clarity of the filtered water. (Fig. 4)

Fig. 3: Which filter do you think will work best?

CREATIVE ENRICHMENT

Plant chia seeds or grass on topsoil in one of the filters to test how plant roots contribute to filtration. Test the filters every week for several weeks as the roots get longer.

THE SCIENCE BEHIND THE FUN

Healthy soil is an important water filter. Rock, sand, silt, clay, water, air, and organic matter such as decaying plants are some of the components that make up soil, and it's teeming with life, including bacteria, fungi, arthropods, and worms.

Certain soil components are very good at attracting and holding on to pollutants that flow with water into dirt. Since soil contains small particles such as silt and clay, it is also a good physical filter. Large particles become trapped in the matrix and can't move very far. Microbes in the dirt break down certain pollutants into harmless compounds. Some bacteria can even break down fossil fuels.

In this lab, you "pollute" water with food coloring and run it through soil filters. Although you might expect sand to be a better filter than dirt, this lab might change your mind. You'll also notice that dirt doesn't filter everything out. That's why it's important to be careful about the chemicals we put on our lawns and crops, since some of them get back into the water.

UNIT 12
FROZEN FUN

IF YOU LOOK CLOSELY ENOUGH AT THE CENTER OF A SNOWFLAKE, THERE'S A GOOD CHANCE YOU'LL FIND SOME BACTERIAL DNA.

As temperatures drop, water molecules move more slowly and gather close together, but they need a physical scaffold called a *nucleator* to snap them into the correct arrangement for ice crystal formation. High in the atmosphere, cold water molecules form cages around nucleators including dust, soot, and airborne bacteria, which push them into the correct shape to make ice crystals. Other water molecules can attach to these primary crystals, forming snowflakes. Atmospheric conditions and temperature affect the shape and design of each snowflake that falls to Earth.

Scientists have shown that many microbes are blown high into the atmosphere by winds and can survive the extreme conditions, allowing them to travel widely. When certain ice-crystal catalyzing bacteria need transportation back down to Earth, they spit out special proteins that are exceptionally good nucleators. Whether they hit the ground as raindrops or snowflakes depends on the temperature closer to the ground. Many scientists believe that airborne microbes influence cloud formation and weather.

This chapter gives you some ideas for experimenting in winter and summer. Try snow-melting science, see how cold slows chemical reactions, sculpt volcano cones from snow, taste maple syrup candy, and try your hand at making ice cream.

LAB 48

ICE CREAM KEEP AWAY

MATERIALS

→ 2 cups (475 ml) milk

→ 2 cups (475 ml) heavy cream

→ ½ cup (100 g) sugar

→ 2 tablespoons (30 ml) vanilla

→ Pint or quart (0.5 or 1 L)-size plastic zip-top freezer bags

→ Gallon (3.8 L)-size zip-top freezer bags

→ Large bag of ice

→ 2 cups (576 g) table salt or (480 g) Kosher salt

→ Dish towels

SAFETY TIPS & HINTS

— If the ice cream isn't frozen when you check it, add more ice and salt to the outer bag and continue to throw it around for another 5 or 10 minutes.

TURN THE SCIENCE OF HEAT TRANSFER INTO A SPORT WITH EDIBLE RESULTS.

Fig. 5: Keep away is fun too.

PROTOCOL

STEP 1: Make an ice cream mixture by combining the milk, cream, sugar, and vanilla in a bowl and mixing well. (Fig. 1)

STEP 2: Add 1 cup (235 ml) of the ice cream mixture to a freezer bag, squeeze out some of the air, and zip it closed. Place the small bag of ice cream mixture in a second small bag, squeeze out the air, and zip it closed as well. Place the double-bagged ice cream mixture into a gallon-size (3.8 L) freezer bag and fill the larger bag with ice.

STEP 3: Pour a generous ½ cup (150 g) of salt over the ice in the bag and zip the bag shut. (Fig. 2)

STEP 4: Wrap a dish towel around the bag of ice and place it in a second gallon–size (3.8 L) bag. Zip the outer bag closed. (Fig. 3)

STEP 5: Play catch with the bag of ice and ice cream for 10 to 15 minutes. (Fig. 4, 5)

Fig. 1: Add 1 cup (235 ml) of ice cream mixture to a zip-top freezer bag.

Fig. 2: Put the bagged mix in a larger bag with ice and salt.

Fig. 3: Wrap ice bag in a towel and place it inside another bag.

Fig.4: Play catch with the ice cream mix.

Fig. 6: Remove the bag of ice cream mix from the outer bags.

Fig. 7: Taste your science experiment.

STEP 6: Remove the bag of ice cream mix from the outer bags and enjoy your frozen treat. (Fig. 6, 7)

STEP 7: Repeat steps 2 through 8 with the rest of the ice cream mixture. Or keep the mixture in the refrigerator until you're ready to use it.

CREATIVE ENRICHMENT

Try adding less salt to the ice to freeze the ice cream more slowly. How does this change the texture?

THE SCIENCE BEHIND THE FUN

Making ice cream is a lesson in heat transfer and crystallization. Water is the solid form of ice. When you add salt to ice, it lowers the freezing temperature of the water, melting it and allowing it to remain a liquid far below water's normal freezing temperature of 32°F (0°C).

In this lab, adding salt melts the ice, making a really, really cold ice-salt-water mix. Because heat flows from warmer regions to colder ones, heat is transferred out of the ice cream mixture into the ice water, freezing the water in the ice cream mix into ice crystals.

Depending on how fast ice cream freezes and what ingredients it contains, the ice crystals will be different sizes. If you freeze the mixture very fast, you will probably get big ice crystals that make the ice cream grainy. Agitating the mixture and adding ingredients such as gelatin encourage smaller crystals to form, making smoother frozen treats.

MOUTHWATERING MAPLE CANDY

MATERIALS

→ Fresh, clean snow

→ Flat dish or pan (optional)

→ 1 cup (235 ml) pure maple syrup

→ Saucepan

→ Candy thermometer

→ Heat-resistant measuring cup

→ Fork

→ Sticks or skewers (optional)

MAKE AMAZING MAPLE TREATS USING HEAT EVAPORATION AND QUICK COOLING IN THE SNOW.

Fig. 4: Remove the candy from the snow with a fork.

SAFETY TIPS & HINTS

— Hot sugar syrup can cause burns. This experiment must be done with adult supervision.

— Allow the candy to cool completely before tasting.

— Only use pure maple syrup for the best results.

PROTOCOL

STEP 1: Go outside and scout out a spot with some clean snow several inches (15 to 20 cm) deep for making your candy. Or collect and pack down a few inches (8 to 10 cm) of fresh snow in a large, flat container.

STEP 2: Boil the maple syrup in a saucepan, stirring constantly until it reaches about 235°F to 240°F (113°C to 116°C) on a candy thermometer (soft ball stage). It will take about 6 minutes once the mixture starts to boil. (Fig. 1)

STEP 3: Remove the maple syrup from the heat and carefully pour it into a heat-resistant container with a spout, such as a Pyrex measuring cup.

STEP 4: Pour wiggly candy lines onto the snow to freeze them into shape. You can pour it directly onto the snow outside or snow you've packed into a container, if you prefer. (Fig. 2, 3)

STEP 5: When the shapes have hardened, remove them from the snow with a fork. (Fig. 4, 5)

STEP 6: You can eat your candy right away, or let it warm up and wind it around sticks or skewers.

Fig. 1: Boil the syrup in a saucepan.

Fig. 2: Pour the syrup into the snow to make candy shapes.

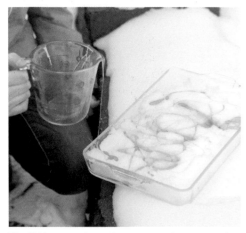

Fig. 3: You can also put some snow in a casserole dish to make your candy.

Fig. 5: Does the cold candy hold its shape?

CREATIVE ENRICHMENT

1. Try collecting some syrup from your pan at several different temperatures and compare the resulting snow candy for texture, color, and consistency.

2. Can you do the same experiment with other sugar syrups, such molasses or corn syrup?

3. Try making maple sugar (see *The Science Behind the Fun*).

THE SCIENCE
BEHIND THE FUN

Maple syrup is made from tree sap that is boiled to evaporate most of its moisture. After evaporation, the syrup that remains is made up mostly of a sugar called *sucrose*, but it also contains smaller amounts of glucose and fructose.

Other organic compounds are also present in tree sap, giving syrup from different areas unique flavors. Syrup collected earlier in spring when it is cold tends to be light in color and have a milder flavor. As the days get warmer, microbes ferment some of the sugar in the syrup, making it darker and giving it a more robust taste.

In this experiment, you heat maple syrup, evaporating even more water. A supersaturated solution forms, which holds more sugar molecules in the liquid than would be possible if you evaporated the water at room temperature.

When you pour the supersaturated sugar into the snow, it cools quickly, forming sugar crystals to give the maple candy a soft, semisolid consistency. Heating the syrup to a higher temperature will evaporate more water, resulting in even more crystal formation in the cooled syrup, making it harder to bite. If you carefully evaporate all of the water from maple syrup, you'll be left with pure maple sugar crystals.

SNOW MELT EXPERIMENT

MATERIALS

→ 1 or 2 buckets or large plastic containers

→ Snow

→ Measuring stick or ruler

→ Science notebook

→ Clear glass or jar

SAFETY TIPS & HINTS

— Never leave young children unattended near water.

— Don't drink the melted snow.

COLLECT A BUCKETFUL OF SNOW TO SEE WHAT'S INSIDE THE WHITE STUFF.

Fig. 2: Measure how deep the snow is.

PROTOCOL

STEP 1: Fill a bucket or container with snow. Level off the snow without packing it down too much. (Fig. 1)

STEP 2: Fill a second container with snow (optional). Pack it down and level it off.

STEP 3: Use a measuring stick to see how deep the snow is in each container and write it down in your science notebook or on a piece of paper. (Fig. 2)

Fig. 1: Collect snow in a container.

Fig. 3: Measure the depth of the melted snow.

STEP 4: Bring the container(s) inside and wait for the snow to melt.

STEP 5: When all the snow has melted into water, measure how deep the water is and record it in your notebook, next to your premelt measurements. (Fig. 3)

STEP 6: Pour some of the water into a clear glass or jar and see how clear it is. Record your observations or take a picture of the water and tape it in your notebook. (Fig. 4)

Fig. 4: Check the clarity of the water from the melted snow.

CREATIVE ENRICHMENT

1. Make bacterial growth medium (see *References*, page 141) and culture some of your snow water to see whether you can grow any microorganisms.

2. Test snow after more than one snowfall and compare water content.

THE SCIENCE BEHIND THE FUN

The term *snow crystal* refers to a single crystal of ice formed when the water vapor in a cloud freezes on the surface of a seed crystal, which has formed on a microbe or piece of dust. Snowflakes can contain several snow crystals stuck together. Sometimes they form large clumps, creating huge, fluffy snowflakes.

Temperature and humidity affect how snowflakes form. Some have long, feathery branches, while others are small and platelike, but they all have six sides, due to the physical properties of water molecules.

The shape of snow crystals, the weather, and the surface where they land all affect how much air is trapped when snow piles up. The amount of air contained in a layer of snow affects its volume, or how much space it takes up.

When snow melts, the trapped air is released. That's why the volume of snow is greater than the volume of the liquid water it forms when it melts.

LAB 51 — FROZEN VOLCANOES

SCULPT A "LAVA"-SPEWING SNOW CONE IN YOUR OWN BACKYARD.

MATERIALS

→ 1 cup (235 ml) vinegar

→ Empty 16- to 20-ounce (about 500 ml) plastic bottle

→ Food coloring

→ Paper funnel or paper cup

→ ¼ cup (55 g) baking soda

→ Snow

SAFETY TIPS & HINTS

— Vinegar is a mild acid and can sting your eyes.

Fig. 4: You've made snow volcanoes!

PROTOCOL

STEP 1: Pour the vinegar into a plastic bottle.

STEP 2: Add a few drops of food coloring to the vinegar. (Fig. 1)

STEP 3: Prepare a paper funnel or squeeze the lip of a paper cup to form a pouring container.

STEP 4: Measure the baking soda into a cup if using a funnel or add it to your paper pouring cup.

Fig. 1: Add vinegar and food coloring to plastic bottles.

Fig. 2: Quickly pour baking soda into the volcano.

STEP 5: Go outside and set your plastic bottle on the ground with the mouth facing up. Form a cone of snow around your plastic bottle so that it looks like a volcano.

STEP 6: Quickly pour all of the baking soda into the bottle using your funnel or pouring container and stand back! (Fig. 2, 3, 4)

Fig. 3: Remove the cone quickly.

CREATIVE ENRICHMENT

1. Try the same experiment using warm vinegar.

2. Do the experiment in a large bottle and calculate how much baking soda and vinegar you'd need for a good eruption from a larger container.

THE SCIENCE BEHIND THE FUN

Chemical reactions occur when you combine two things, such as baking soda and vinegar, to make something new. The chemical name for baking soda is sodium bicarbonate, and scientists call vinegar acetic acid.

One of the products created by combining baking soda and vinegar is carbon dioxide gas. The gas pressure builds rapidly inside the bottle when you add the baking soda, and the only way for the carbon dioxide to escape is through the mouth of the bottle. It escapes with enough force to overcome the force of gravity, and it shoots some liquid into the air along with it before gravity pulls it back down to earth.

In Iceland, there are many active volcanoes buried under snow, ice, and even glaciers. When they erupt, ash often covers the snow before the lava flow arrives. When hot lava meets snow and ice, hissing steam erupts into the air. Some scientists believe that lava flows actually move more quickly over ice than they do over dry land.

LAB 52

COLD-AIR BALLOONS

MATERIALS

→ 2 identical empty plastic water bottles

→ ²/₃ cup (160 ml) vinegar

→ 2 identical medium-size balloons

→ Spoon or paper funnel

→ 6 teaspoons (28 g) baking soda

→ Measuring cup with spout (optional)

SAFETY TIPS & HINTS

— You'll need two people to do this experiment, so you can start the reactions at the same time.

— Vinegar is a mild acid that can sting your eyes. Use caution when microwaving it.

— Small children may need assistance filling balloons with baking soda.

HAVE AN INFLATION RACE TO TEST WHETHER HOT OR COLD CHEMICAL REACTIONS BLOW UP BALLOONS FASTER.

Fig. 4: See which balloon inflates faster.

PROTOCOL

STEP 1: Label one bottle "warm" and the other bottle "cold."

STEP 2: Add exactly ⅓ cup (80 ml) vinegar to the empty plastic bottle labeled "cold." Set the bottle in the snow, outside in the cold, or in the freezer for 30 minutes to chill the vinegar.

STEP 3: After your "cold" bottle has chilled for 30 minutes, heat the remaining ⅓ cup (80 ml) vinegar in the microwave for about 30 seconds until it is warm but not hot. Add it to your other bottle, labeled "warm."

STEP 4: Stretch out the balloons to loosen them up a bit. Use a spoon or paper funnel to carefully measure 3 teaspoons (14 g) of the baking soda into each uninflated balloon. Shake the baking soda to the bottom of the balloons. (Fig. 1)

STEP 5: Take both bottles outside, along with your baking soda–filled balloons. Stretch the mouth of a balloon over each bottle, being careful not to spill baking soda into the bottles. (Fig. 2)

Fig. 1: Add the baking soda to the balloons.

Fig. 2: Put a baking soda-filled balloon on each bottle.

STEP 6: With one person at each bottle of vinegar, start the chemical reactions by shaking all of the baking soda from the balloons into the vinegar in both bottles, simultaneously. Hold the balloon on the mouth of each bottle as it inflates with carbon dioxide gas. (Fig. 3)

STEP 7: See which balloon inflates faster. (Fig. 4)

Fig. 3: Shake the baking soda into each bottle simultaneously.

CREATIVE ENRICHMENT

1. Tell someone why it's important to use the same size containers and same quantities of reagents for this experiment.

2. Repeat the experiment with frozen vinegar as one of the variables. What else could you do to change the reaction rates?

3. Repeat the experiment several times, simultaneously removing both balloons from the bottles after five, ten, fifteen, and thirty seconds from the reaction start time and tying them. Weigh or measure the balloons to calculate the difference in the amount of inflation with carbon dioxide gas over time.

THE SCIENCE BEHIND THE FUN

Mixing different kinds of molecules together to make something new is called a *chemical reaction*. When you mix together sodium bicarbonate (baking soda) and dilute acetic acid (vinegar), you make carbon dioxide gas. In this experiment, the gas is trapped in bottles, and the pressure from the gas inflates the balloons.

When you heat a substance, molecules start to move around faster and tend to bump into each other more often and with more energy. For most chemical reactions to occur, molecules have to be moving fast enough to collide with a certain amount of energy, called *activation energy*.

When you add warm vinegar to baking soda, the chemical reaction occurs very quickly, inflating the balloon faster than the same chemical reaction started with cold vinegar did.

Hazel Kate Lucy Cam Sarah Lily Grey Cela Tess

Scarlett Ella Eva Nora AJ Katherine Lilly Lily Yara

Mina Aryanna Darya Maya Isaac Knox Bristow Emily Kendall

Stephan Mikaylah Wyatt Owen Elena Grace Charlie Grace Mary Ruth

Frances Claire George Jack Connor James Amelie April Will

Sam Nick Chloe Ryan Tom Hema Lara Cate Natalie

Ella Carlo Enzo Seth Christopher Sam Kyra Sarah Carissa

Molly Sophia Geneva Charlie John Georgia Elena May Hailey

RESOURCES

ALL THINGS SPACE AND EARTH SCIENCE
www.nasa.gov

BUTTERFLIES
www.monarchwatch.org
en.butterflycorner.net

CITIZEN SCIENCE
scistarter.com

CLIMATE SCIENCE
climate.nasa.gov
climatekids.nasa.gov

EARTHWORMS
www.greatlakeswormwatch.org

FRESHWATER MACROINVERTEBRATE IDENTIFICATION
www.vitalsignsme.org/macroinvertebrates
www.stroudcenter.org

GENERAL CHEMISTRY
acswebcontent.acs.org/scienceforkids

MOSS
www.youtube.com/watch?v=Z9AdP1PoImE

PLANT IDENTIFICATION
www.leafsnap.com

ROCKET SCIENCE
www.jpl.nasa.gov/edu
www.nasa.gov/audience/forkids/kidsclub/flash/index.html

SOLAR SCIENCE
solarscience.msfc.nasa.gov
www.northernlightscentre.ca

SUPERCOOLED WATER VIDEO
www.youtube.com/watch?v=XWR5d7C0hZs

TADPOLES
www.pwrc.usgs.gov/tadpole

TARDIGRADES
www.americanscientist.org/issues/feature/tardigrades

TARDIGRADE VIDEO
www.youtube.com/watch?v=H5nnrWuyHAU

WAVE SCIENCE VIDEO
www.youtube.com/watch?v=z-_4k5y7Vjg

ACKNOWLEDGMENTS

Without my family and friends, this book wouldn't exist. Thank you especially to the following people:

My science consultant, Ron Lee, who suggested several of the experiments in this book and made sure that I explained the physics correctly. Not only is he brilliant, he's my dad.

My kids, Sarah, May, and Charlie, and my husband, Ken, who helped out with numerous photo shoots and spent the summer in a house that looked like a science fair gone wrong.

Holly Lipelt and Lali Garcia DeRosier, who shared some of their students' favorite biology experiments with me, and Dr. Raychelle Burks, for making sure I got the chemistry of lip balm right. Greg Heinecke, my education adviser, who told me what teachers want to see in a book.

Richardson Nature Center in Bloomington, Minnesota, where we netted insects with the naturalist Heidi Matheson Wolter and were guided on a spectacular full-moon hike by naturalist Pauline Bold. Thank you to Michael Gottschalk for coordinating.

Marion McNurlen, our neighborhood monarch guru, who raises a kaleidoscope of butterflies on her porch every summer and inspires us to learn more about their plight.

The Bakken Museum of Electricity and Magnetism in Minneapolis, Minnesota, for letting us catch tadpoles in their fountain.

My incessantly cheerful photographer Amber Procaccini, who braved mud, worms, and rough terrain to create the fantastic photographs in this book.

Jennifer, Karen, Tim, and Molly who let us invade their backyards with hordes of young experimenters for the sake of science.

The amazing, smart, funny, and beautiful kids whose smiles light up the pages of this book.

Jonathan Simcosky, Renae Haines, David Martinell, Katie Fawkes, Lisa Trudeau, and the entire team at Quarry Books for your helpfulness, patience, and creativity.

And my mom, Jean Lee, who always made me go outside to play.

ABOUT THE AUTHOR

Liz Heinecke has loved science since she was old enough to inspect her first caterpillar.

After working in molecular biology research for ten years, she left the lab to kick off a new chapter in her life as a stay-at-home mom. Soon she found herself sharing her love of science with her three kids and journaling their experiments and adventures on her Kitchen Pantry Scientist website.

Her enthusiasm for science soon led to regular appearances on Twin Cities television stations, the creation of the KidScience app, and the publication of her first book, *Kitchen Science Lab for Kids: 52 Family-Friendly Experiments from Around the House* (Quarry Books, 2014).

When she's not driving her kids around, you'll find Liz at home in Minnesota doing science outreach and communication, experimenting, writing, singing, playing banjo, painting, running, and doing almost anything else to avoid housework.

She graduated from Luther College where she studied art and biology. Liz received her master's degree in bacteriology from the University of Wisconsin, Madison.

ABOUT THE PHOTOGRAPHER

Amber Procaccini is a commercial and editorial photographer based in Minneapolis, Minnesota. She specializes in photographing kids, babies, food, and travel, and her passion for photography almost equals her passion for finding the perfect taco. Amber met Liz while photographing her first book, *Kitchen Science Lab for Kids,* and she knew they'd make a great team when they bonded over cornichons, pate, and brie. When Amber isn't photographing eye-rolling tweens or making cheeseburgers look sexy, she and her husband love to travel and enjoy new adventures together.

ALSO AVAILABLE

Gardening Lab for Kids
978-1-59253-904-8

Kitchen Science Lab for Kids
978-1-59253-925-3

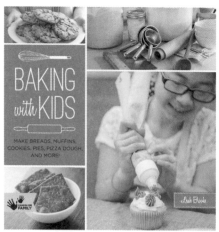

Baking with Kids
978-1-59253-977-2

Paint Lab for Kids
978-1-63159-078-8